S P  W9-BSK-328

MAINE'S SOUTHERN COAST

HILARY NANGLE

Contents

MAINE'S
SOUTHERN COAST

© EDELLA/123RF.COM

SOUTHERN COAST

Drive over the I-95 bridge from New Hampshire into Maine's Southern Coast region on a bright summer day and you'll swear the air is cleaner, the sky is bluer, the trees are greener, and the roadside signs are more upbeat—"Welcome to Maine: The Way Life Should Be." (Or is it the way life *used* to be?)

Most visitors come to this region for the spectacular attractions of the justly world-famous Maine coast—the inlets, villages, and especially the beaches—but it's also rich in history. Southernmost York County, part of the Province of Maine, was incorporated in 1636, only 16 years after the *Mayflower* pilgrims reached Plymouth, Massachusetts, and reeks of history: ancient cemeteries, musty archives,

and architecturally stunning homes and public buildings. Probably the best places to dive into that history are the sites of the Old York Historical Society in York Harbor.

Geological fortune smiled on this 50-mile ribbon, endowing it with a string of sandy beaches—nirvana for sun worshippers but less enchanting to swimmers, who need to steel themselves to be able to spend much time in the ocean, especially in early summer before the water temperature has reached a tolerable level.

Complementing those beaches are amusement parks and arcades, fishing shacks-turned-chic boutiques, a surprising number of good restaurants given the region's seasonality, and some of the state's prettiest parks and

© HILARY NANGLE

HIGHLIGHTS

LOOK FOR ◖ TO FIND RECOMMENDED SIGHTS, ACTIVITIES, DINING, AND LODGING.

◖ **Old York Historical Society:** York dates from the 1640s, and on this campus of historic buildings you can peek into early life in the area (page 16).

◖ **Nubble Light and Sohier Park:** You'll likely recognize this often-photographed Maine Coast icon, which is the easiest lighthouse to see in the region (page 16).

◖ **Ogunquit Museum of American Art:** It's hard to say which is more jaw-dropping, the art or the view (page 25).

◖ **Marginal Way:** Escape the hustle and bustle of Ogunquit with a stroll on this paved shorefront path (page 25).

◖ **Wells Reserve at Laudholm Farm:** Orient yourself at the visitors center, where you can learn about the history, flora, and fauna, and then take a leisurely walk to the seashore, passing through a variety of habitats (page 26).

◖ **Seashore Trolley Museum:** Ding-ding-ding goes the bell, and zing-zing-zing go your heartstrings, especially if you're a trolley fan (page 37).

◖ **Dock Square:** Brave the shopping crowds and browse the dozens of fish shacks-turned-boutiques in the heart of Kennebunkport (page 40).

◖ **St. Anthony's Franciscan Monastery:** It's hard to believe this oasis of calm is just a short stroll from busy-busy Dock Square (page 40).

◖ **Wood Island Lighthouse:** Tour Maine's second-oldest lighthouse and perhaps even climb the tower (page 55).

preserves. Spend some time poking around the small villages that give the region so much character. Many have been gussied up and gentrified quite a bit yet retain their seafaring or farming bones.

Some Mainers refer to the Southern Coast as northern Massachusetts. Sometimes it can seem that way, not only for the numbers of Massachusetts plates in evidence but also because many former Massachusetts residents have moved here for the quality of life but continue to commute to jobs in the Boston area. The resulting downside is escalating real-estate prices that have forced families off land that has been in their families for generations and pushed those in traditional seafaring occupations inland. Still, if you nose around and get off the beaten path, you'll find that real Maine is still here.

PLANNING YOUR TIME

Maine's Southern Coast is a rather compact

region, but it's heavily congested, especially in summer. Still, with a minimum of four days, you should be able to take in most of the key sights, including beaches and museums, as long as you don't spend too many hours basking in the sun.

Route 1, the region's primary artery, often has bumper-to-bumper traffic. If you're hopscotching towns, consider using I-95, which has exits for York, Kennebunk, and Saco-Biddeford-Old Orchard Beach. Parking can also be a challenge and expensive, but a trolley system operates in summer and connects most towns, making it easy to avoid the hassles and help the environment.

July and August are the busiest months, with the best beach weather. Spring and fall are lovely, and most attractions are open. In winter, you can walk the beaches without running into another soul, it's easy to get dinner reservations, and lodging prices plummet; the trade-off is that fewer businesses are open.

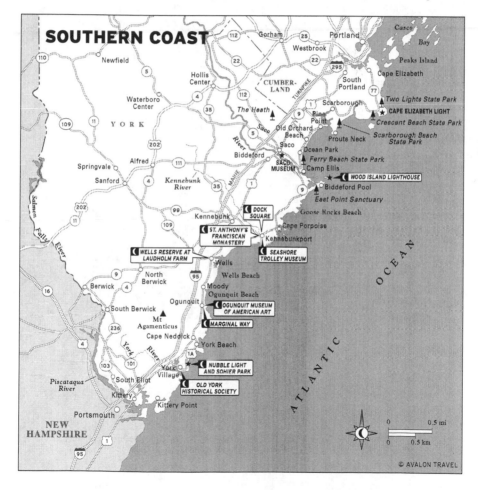

© AVALON TRAVEL

Kittery

Maine is home to a lot of well-kept secrets, Kittery (pop. 9,490) being one of them. Shoppers rarely get beyond the 120-plus outlets along Route 1, but there's equal value in exploring the back roads of Maine's oldest town, settled in 1623 and chartered in 1647. Parks, a small nautical museum, historic architecture, and foodie finds are only a few of the attractions in Kittery and its "suburb," **Kittery Point.** It was also on Kittery's Badger Island where the sloop *Ranger* was launched in 1777. The shipbuilding continues at Portsmouth Naval Shipyard on Kittery's Dennet's Island, the first government shipyard in the United States.

SIGHTS

Avoid the outlet sprawl and see the prettiest part of the area by driving along squiggly Route 103 from the Route 1 traffic circle in Kittery through Kittery Point (administratively part of Kittery) and on to Route 1A in York. You can even make a day of it, stopping at the sights mentioned here. Be very careful to watch for cyclists and pedestrians, as there are no shoulders and lots of blind corners and hills.

Kittery Historical and Naval Museum

Maritime history buffs shouldn't miss the small but well-stocked Kittery Historical and Naval Museum (200 Rogers Rd. Ext., near the junction of Rte. 1 and Rte. 236, Kittery, 207/439-3080, www.kitterymuseum.com, 10am-4pm Tues.-Sat. June-Oct., $5 adults, $3 ages 7-15, $10 family). A large exhibit hall and a small back room contain ship models, fishing gear, old photos and paintings, and an astonishing collection of scrimshaw (carved whale ivory).

Lady Pepperrell House

The 1760 Georgian Lady Pepperrell House (Pepperrell Rd./Rte. 103, just before the Fort McClary turnoff, Kittery Point) is privately owned and not open to the public, but it's worth admiring from afar. Nearby, across from the First Congregational Church, is the area's most-visited burying ground. Old-cemetery buffs should bring rubbing gear here for some interesting grave markers. The tomb of Levi Thaxter (husband of poet Celia Thaxter) bears an epitaph written for him by Robert Browning.

Fort McClary Historic Site

Since the early 18th century, fortifications have stood on this 27-acre headland protecting

Fort McClary has guarded Portsmouth Harbor since the early 18th century.

© TOM NANGLE

Portsmouth Harbor from seaborne foes. Contemporary remnants at Fort McClary (Rte. 103, Kittery Point, 207/439-2845, daily, $3 nonresident adults, $2 Maine adults, $1 ages 5-11 and nonresident seniors, free resident seniors) include several outbuildings, an 1846 blockhouse, granite walls, and earthworks—all with a view of Portsmouth Harbor. Opposite are the sprawling buildings of the Portsmouth Naval Shipyard. Bring a picnic (covered tables and a lily pond are across the street) and turn the kids loose to run and play. It's officially open May 30-October 1, but the site is accessible in the off-season. The fort is 2.5 miles east of Route 1.

Fort Foster

The only problem with Fort Foster (Pocahontas Rd., off Rte. 103, Gerrish Island, Kittery Point, 207/439-3800, 10am-8pm daily late May-early Sept., 10am-8pm Sat.-Sun. May and Sept., $10 vehicle pass, $5 adult walk-in, $1 child walk-in) is that it's no secret, so parking can be scarce at this 90-acre municipal park at the entrance to Portsmouth Harbor. On a hot day, arrive early. You can swim, hike the nature trails, fish off the pier (state registration required for age 16 and older), picnic, and investigate the tidepools. Bring a kite; there's almost always a breeze.

ENTERTAINMENT

Kittery Recreation (207/439-3800, www.kittery.org) presents a **summer concert series** on the common, which varies year to year; most of the concerts are free.

SHOPPING

There is no question that you'll find bargains at Kittery's 120-plus factory outlets (www.thekitteryoutlets.com), which are actually a bunch of mini-malls clustered along Route 1. All the household names are here: Bass, Calvin Klein, Eddie Bauer, J. Crew, Mikasa, Esprit, Lenox, Timberland, Tommy Hilfiger, Gap, Villeroy & Boch, and plenty more (all open daily). Anchoring it all is the **Kittery Trading Post** (301 Rte. 1, Kittery, 207/439-2700 or 888/587-6246, www.kitterytradingpost.com), a humongous sporting-goods and clothing emporium. Try to avoid the outlets on weekends, when you might need to take a number for the fitting rooms.

RECREATION
Brave Boat Harbor

One of the Rachel Carson National Wildlife Refuge's 11 Maine coastal segments is Brave Boat Harbor (207/646-9226), a beautifully unspoiled 560-acre wetlands preserve in Kittery Point. There are hiking trails, but the habitat is particularly sensitive here, so be kind to the environment. Take Route 103 to Chauncey Creek Road and continue past the Gerrish Island bridge to Cutts Island Lane. Just beyond it and across a small bridge is a pullout on the left. You have a couple of options for hikes: a 1.8-mile loop trail, including a spur, or a half-mile loop. Bring binoculars to spot waterfowl in the marshlands.

Captain and Patty's Piscataqua River Tours

Take a spin around the Piscataqua River Basin with Captain and Patty's Piscataqua River Tours (Town Dock, Pepperrell Rd., Kittery Point, 207/439-3655, www.capandpatty.com, $19 adults, $10 under age 10). The 80-minute historical tour aboard an open launch departs six times daily. En route, Captain Neil Odams points out historic forts, lighthouses, and the Naval Shipyard.

ACCOMMODATIONS

Rates reflect peak season.

Put a little ooh and aah into your touring with a visit to the **Portsmouth Harbor Inn and Spa** (6 Water St., Kittery, 207/439-4040, www.innatportsmouth.com, $165-195). The handsome brick inn, built in 1889, looks out over the Piscataqua River, Portsmouth, and the Portsmouth Naval Shipyard. Five attractive Victorian-style guest rooms, most with water views, are furnished with antiques and have air-conditioning, TVs, Wi-Fi, and phones. There's an outdoor hot tub, and beach chairs are available. Breakfasts are multicourse feasts. Request a back room if you're noise sensitive, although air-conditioning camouflages traffic noise in summer. Rooms on the third floor have the best views, but these also have handheld showers. Now for the "aah" part: The inn also has a full-service spa.

FOOD

Days and hours of operation reflect peak season and are subject to change.

Local Flavors

Kittery has an abundance of excellent specialty food stores that are perfect for stocking up for a picnic lunch or dinner. Most are along the section of Route 1 between the Portsmouth bridge and the traffic circle, and three are within steps of one another. At **Beach Pea Baking Co.** (53 Rte. 1, Kittery, 207/439-3555, www.beachpeabaking.com, 7:30am-6pm Mon.-Sat.) you can buy fabulous breads and pastries. Sandwiches and salads are made to order 11am-3pm daily. There's pleasant seating indoors and on a patio. Next door is **Golden Harvest** (47 State Rd./Rte. 1, 207/439-2113, 7am-6:30pm Mon.-Sat., 9am-6pm Sun.), where you can load up on luscious produce. Across the street is **Terra Cotta Pasta Co.** (52 Rte. 1, 207/475-3025, www.terracottapastacompany.com, 10am-6pm Mon., 9am-6:30pm Tues.-Sat., 10:30am-5pm Sun.), where in addition to handmade pastas you'll find salads, soups, sandwiches, prepared foods, and lots of other goodies.

Let your nose guide you into Byrne & Carlson (60 Rte. 1, Kittery, 888/559-9778, www.byrneandcarlson.com), which makes elegant and delicious chocolate for connoisseurs.

Here's a twofold find. **When Pigs Fly** (460 Rte. 1, Kittery, 207/438-7036, www.sendbread.com) earned renown for its Old World artisanal breads made from organic ingredients. Now it's also home to **When Pigs Fly Wood-Fired Pizzeria** (11:30am-9pm Sun.-Thurs., to 10pm Fri.-Sat., $12-22). Of course there's pizza—-Neopolitan style in creative flavor combos—but there are other choices, including house-made charcuterie.

Want a down-home breakfast or lunch? The **Sunrise Grill** (182 State Rd./Rte. 1, Kittery traffic circle, Kittery, 207/439-5748, www.sunrisegrillinc.com, 6:30am-2pm daily, $5-13) delivers with waffles, granola, omelets, Diana's Benedict, salads, sandwiches, and burgers.

Casual Dining

The commitment to using fresh and local foods and the flair for bringing big flavors out of simple ingredients have earned 【 **Anneke Jans** (60 Wallingford Sq., Kittery, 207/439-0001, www.annekejans.net, from 5pm daily, $17-35) kudos far beyond Kittery. Signature dishes include mussels prepared with bacon, shallots, and bleu cheese, available as an appetizer or entrée. This is a local hot spot with a lively crowd; reservations are recommended. Gluten-free options are available.

Farm-to-table meets gastropub at **The Black Birch** (2 Government St., Kittery, 207/703-2294, www.theblackbirch.com, 3:30pm-10pm Tues.-Thurs., to 11pm Fri.-Sat., $7-19). Upscale comfort foods, such as bacon and bleu cheese mac, poutine and duck confit, and white corn polenta fries, are presented in a menu designed to mix and match, accompanied by a geek-worthy beer list.

Ignore the kitschy lighthouse; **Robert's Maine Grill** (326 Rte. 1, Kittery, 207/439-0300, www.robertsmainegrill.com, from 11:30pm daily, $16-25) is a fine place to duck out of the shopping madness and enjoy well-prepared seafood that goes far beyond the usual fried choices, as well as a few landlubber options. Kids' menu available.

Ethnic Fare

Craving Cal-Mex? Some of the recipes in Luis Valdez's **Loco Coco's Tacos** (36 Walker St., Kittery, 207/438-9322, www.locococos.com, 11am-8pm Mon.-Wed., to 9pm Thurs.-Sat., 10am-8pm Sun.) have been passed down for generations, and the homemade salsas have flavor and kick. If you're feeling really decadent, go for the artery-busting California fries. There are gluten-free and kids' menus, too. Most choices are less than $10. Choose from self-serve, dining room, or bar seating.

Chef Rajesh Mandekar blends techniques drawn from Indian, French, and Italian cuisines to create rave-worthy Indian fare at **Tulsi** (20 Walker St., Kittery, 207/451-9511, www. tulsiindianrestaurant.com, 5pm-10pm Tues.-Sat., noon-2:30pm and 5pm-9pm Sun., $9-22).

Lobster and Clams

If you came to Maine to eat lobster, **Chauncey Creek Lobster Pier** (16 Chauncey Creek Rd., off Rte. 103, Kittery Point, 207/439-1030, www.chaunceycreek.com, 11am-8pm daily mid-May-early Sept., to 7pm daily early Sept.-Columbus Day) is the real deal. Step up to the window, place your order, take a number, and grab a table (you may need to share) overlooking tidal Chauncey Creek and the woods on the close-in opposite shore. It's a particularly picturesque—and extremely popular—place; parking is a nightmare. BYOB and anything else that's not on the menu.

If clams are high on your must-have list, pay a visit to **Bob's Clam Hut** (315 Rte. 1, Kittery, 207/439-4233, www.bobsclamhut. com, from 11am daily, $10-23), next to the Kittery Trading Post. An institution in these parts since 1956, Bob's is *the* place for fried

seafood, especially clams; the tartar sauce is the secret weapon.

GETTING THERE AND AROUND

Kittery is 60 miles or just over an hour via I-95 from Boston, although it can take longer in summer when traffic backs up at tolls. It's about eight miles or 15 minutes via I-95. Allow about 20 minutes via Route 1, to York, although traffic can be bumper-to-bumper in the stretch by the outlets.

EXCURSIONS FROM KITTERY
The Berwicks

Probably the best known of the area's present-day inland communities is the riverside town of South Berwick, thanks to a historical and literary tradition dating to the 17th century, with antique cemeteries to prove it. The 19th- and 20th-century novels of Sarah Orne Jewett and Gladys Hasty Carroll have lured many a contemporary visitor to explore their rural settings, an area aptly described by Carroll as "a small patch of earth continually occupied but never crowded for more than three hundred years."

A ramble through the Berwicks—South Berwick and its siblings—makes a nice diversion from the coast, and because it's off most visitors' radar screens, it's a good alternative for lodging and dining too.

SIGHTS

Don't blink or you might miss the tiny sign outside the 1774 **Sarah Orne Jewett House** (5 Portland St./Rte. 4, South Berwick, 207/384-2454, www.historicnewengland.org, 11am-5pm Fri.-Sun. June 1-Oct. 15, $5) smack in the center of town. Park on the street and join one of the tours to learn details of the Jewett family and its star, Sarah (1849-1909), author of *The Country of the Pointed Firs,* a New England classic. Books by and about her are available in the gift shop. House tours are at 11am and 1,

SOUTHERN COAST

© TOM NANGLE

Sarah Orne Jewett House, South Berwick

2, 3, and 4pm. The house is one of two local Historic New England properties.

The other property is the 18th-century **Hamilton House** (40 Vaughan's Lane, South Berwick, 207/384-2454, www.historicneweng-land.org, 11am-5pm Wed.-Sun. June 1-Oct. 15, $8), which crowns a bluff overlooking the Salmon Falls River and is flanked by handsome Colonial Revival gardens. Knowledgeable guides relate the house's fascinating history. Tours begin only on the hour, the last at 4pm. In July the **Sunday in the Garden** concert series takes place on the lawn ($10, includes a free pass to come back and see the house). Pray for sun; the concert is moved indoors on rainy days. From Route 236 at the southern edge of South Berwick (watch for a signpost), turn left onto Brattle Street and take the second right onto Vaughan's Lane.

Also here is the 150-acre hilltop campus of **Berwick Academy,** Maine's oldest prep school,

chartered in 1791 with John Hancock's signature. The coed school's handsome gray-stone William H. Fogg Memorial Library ("The Fogg") is named for the same family connected with Harvard's Fogg Art Museum. The building's highlight is an incredible collection of dozens of 19th-century stained-glass windows, most designed by Victorian artist Sarah Wyman Whitman, who also designed jackets for Sarah Orne Jewett's books. Thanks to a diligent fund-raising effort, the windows have been restored to their former glory.

RECREATION

When you're ready to stretch your legs, head to **Vaughan Woods State Park** (28 Oldfields Rd., South Berwick, 207/384-5160, 9am-8pm daily late May-early Sept., park trails accessible year-round, $3 adults, $1 ages 5-11, free over age 65 or under age 5) and wander along the three miles of trails in the 250-acre riverside preserve. It adjoins Hamilton House and is connected via a path, but there's far more parking at the park itself.

ENTERTAINMENT

Another reason to venture inland is to catch a production at the **Hackmatack Playhouse** (538 School St./Rte. 9, Berwick, 207/698-1807, www.hackmatack.org), midway between North Berwick and Berwick. The popular summer theater, operating since 1972, is based in a renovated barn reminiscent of a past era and has 8pm performances Wednesday-Saturday, a 2pm matinee Thursday, and children's shows. Tickets are $25 adults, $22 seniors, $10 younger than 20.

ACCOMMODATIONS

These two inns are sleepers (sorry, couldn't resist). Both are within easy striking distance of the coast yet provide far more value than similar properties in the name communities.

Once the headmaster's residence for nearby Berwick Academy, the elegant turn-of-the-20th-century **Academy Street Inn Bed and Breakfast** (15 Academy St., South Berwick, 207/384-5633, year-round, $105-130) has crystal chandeliers, leaded-glass windows, working fireplaces, and high ceilinged rooms full of antiques. Paul and Lee Fopeano's handsome home has five guest rooms with private baths. Full breakfast or afternoon lemonade on the 60-foot screened porch is a real treat.

Innkeepers Ben Gumm and Sally McLaren have turned the outstanding 25-room Queen Anne-style Hurd mansion into the **Angel of the Berwicks** (2 Elm St., North Berwick, 207/676-2133, www.angeloftheberwicks.com,

$119-159), an elegant antiques-filled inn. The property, listed on the National Register of Historic Places, has 11-foot ceilings, stained-glass windows, hand-carved friezes, and ornate mantelpieces. There's even a baby grand piano in the music room. Rates include a full breakfast.

FOOD

A local institution since 1960, **Fogarty's** (471 Main St., South Berwick, 207/384-8361, www.fogartysrestaurant.net, 11am-8pm daily) has expanded through the years from a simple take-out place to a local favorite for inexpensive, family-friendly dining. Ask for a riverview table in the back room.

Far jazzier is **Pepperland Café** (279 Main St., South Berwick, 207/384-5535, www.pepperlandcafe.com, noon-8pm Tues.-Sat., 9am-3pm Sun.), a family-friendly pub-meets-bistro serving comfort food with pizzazz. Make a meal from smaller plates and salads ($8-10) or go big with the entrées ($17-24).

Relish (404 Main St., South Berwick, 207/384-8249, 5:30pm-9pm Wed.-Sat., $18-28) is an intimate, low-key neighborhood bistro where Linda Robinson and Christine Prunier serve well-crafted dinners with a French accent. A gluten-free menu is available. Make reservations: It's worth it.

GETTING THERE

For an easy day trip, loop northwest on Route 236 from Kittery or Route 91 from York to South Berwick, on the New Hampshire border; continue northeast on Route 236 to Berwick, and then head northeast on Route 9 to North Berwick. Continue on Route 9 to return to Wells and the coast.

The Yorks

Four villages with distinct personalities—upscale **York Harbor,** historic **York Village,** casual **York Beach,** and semirural **Cape Neddick**—make up the Town of York (pop. 12,529). First inhabited by Native Americans, who named it Agamenticus, the area was settled as early as 1624, so history is serious business here. High points were its founding by Sir Ferdinando Gorges and the arrival of well-to-do vacationers in the 19th century. In between were Indian massacres, economic woes, and population shuffles. The town's population explodes in summer, which is pretty obvious in July-August when you're searching for a free patch of York Beach sand or a parking place. York Beach, with its seasonal surf and souvenir shops and amusements, has long been the counterpoint to genteel York Village, but that's changing with the restoration and rebirth of York Beach's downtown buildings and the arrival of tony restaurants, shops, and condos.

History and genealogy buffs can study the headstones in the Old Burying Ground or comb the archives of the Old York Historical Society. For lighthouse fans, there are Cape Neddick Light Station ("Nubble Light") and Boon Island, six miles offshore. You can rent horses or mountain bikes on Mount Agamenticus, board a deep-sea fishing boat in York Harbor, or spend an hour hiking the Cliff Path in York Harbor. For the kids there's a zoo, a lobster-boat cruise, a taffy maker, and, of course, the beach.

SIGHTS
◖ Old York Historical Society
Based in York Village, the Old York Historical Society (207 York St., York Village, 207/363-4974, www.oldyork.org, museum buildings 10am-5pm Mon.-Sat. early June-mid-Oct., $12 adults or $6 one building, $10 seniors or

$5 one building, $5 ages 4-16 or $3 one building, $25 family or $15 one building) is the driving force behind a collection of eight colonial and postcolonial buildings plus a research library open throughout the summer. Start at the Jefferds' Tavern Visitor Center (5 Lindsay Rd., York Village), where you'll need to buy tickets. Don't miss the Old Burying Ground, dating from 1735, across the street (rubbings are not allowed). Nearby are the Old Gaol and the School House (both fun for kids), Ramsdell House, and the Emerson-Wilcox House. About 0.5 mile down Lindsay Road on the York River are the John Hancock Warehouse and the George Marshall Store Gallery (140 Lindsay Rd.), operated in the summer as a respected contemporary-art gallery; across the river is the Elizabeth Perkins House. Antiques buffs shouldn't miss the Wilcox and Perkins Houses. These two and the Ramsdell House are open by guided tour; other buildings are self-guided. Visit some or all of the buildings at your own pace; no one leads you from one to another. You can walk to some of the sites from the tavern; to reach others you'll need a car, and parking may be limited.

◖ Nubble Light and Sohier Park
The best-known photo op in York is the distinctive 1879 lighthouse known formally as Cape Neddick Light Station, familiarly "The Nubble." Although there's no access to the lighthouse's island, the Sohier Park Welcome Center (Nubble Rd., off Rte. 1A, between Long and Short Sands Beaches, York Beach, 207/363-7608, www.nubblelight.org, 9am-7pm daily mid-May-mid-Oct.) provides the perfect viewpoint (and has restrooms). Parking is limited, but the turnover is fairly good. It's not a bad idea, however, to walk from the Long Sands parking area or come by bike, even though the

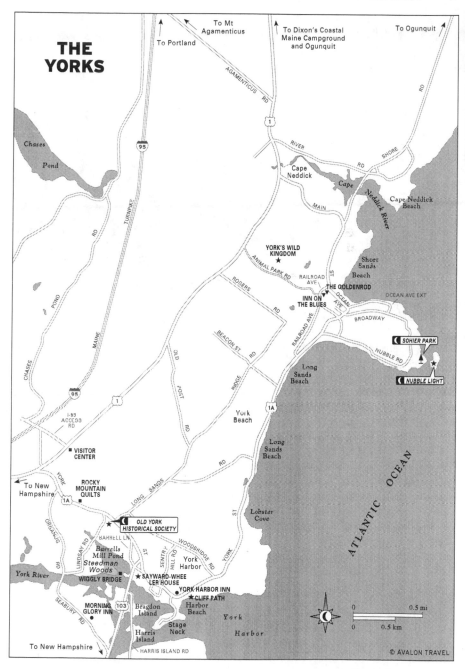

THE YORKS

To Mt Agamenticus
To Portland
To Dixon's Coastal Maine Campground and Ogunquit
To Ogunquit

AGAMENTICUS RD

Chases Pond

95

RIVER RD

SHORE

Cape Neddick

Cape

Neddick River

Cape Neddick Beach

MAIN

TURNPIKE RD

POND RD

MAINE

YORK'S WILD KINGDOM ★

ANIMAL PARK RD

ROGERS RD

RAILROAD AVE

Short Sands Beach

1ST

THE GOLDENROD ▲

INN ON THE BLUES ▲

OCEAN AVE

OCEAN AVE EXT

BEACON ST

OLD POST RD

RIDGE RD

RAILROAD AVE

BROADWAY

◖ **SOHIER PARK**

NUBBLE RD

▲

★

◖ **NUBBLE LIGHT**

CHASES

95

1

I-95 ACCESS RD

Long Sands Beach

York Beach

1A

Long Sands Beach

■ **VISITOR CENTER**

POST RD

■ **ROCKY MOUNTAIN QUILTS**

To New Hampshire

1A

LONG SANDS RD

Lobster Cove

ST

ORGANUG

★ ◖ **OLD YORK HISTORICAL SOCIETY**

BARRELL LN

LINDSAY RD

Barrells Mill Pond

Steedman Woods

■ **WIGGLY BRIDGE**

ST

SENTRY

HILL RD

WOODBRIDGE RD

York Harbor

YORK ST

ATLANTIC OCEAN

RD

York River

★ **SAYWARD-WHEE LER HOUSE**

● **YORK HARBOR INN**

★ **CLIFF PATH**

SEABURY RD

■ **MORNING GLORY INN**

103

Bragdon Island

Harbor Beach

York

Harbor

Stage Neck

Harris Island

To New Hampshire

HARRIS ISLAND RD

0   0.5 mi

0   0.5 km

© AVALON TRAVEL

© TOM NANGLE

The Old Gaol is one of the sites maintained by the Old York Historical Society.

road has inadequate shoulders. Weekdays this is also a popular spot for scuba divers.

Sayward-Wheeler House

Owned by the Boston-based Historic New England, the 1718 Sayward-Wheeler House (9 Barrell Lane Ext., York Harbor, 207/384-2454, www.historicnewengland.org, $5) occupies a prime site at the edge of York Harbor. It's open with tours on the hour 11am-4pm the second and fourth Saturday of the month June-mid-October. In the house are original period furnishings, all in excellent condition. Take Route 1A to Lilac Lane (Rte. 103) to Barrell Lane and then to Barrell Lane Extension, or access it from the Fisherman's Walk.

York's Wild Kingdom

More than 250 creatures—including tigers, zebras, llamas, deer, lions, elephants, and monkeys—find a home at York's Wild Kingdom (102 Railroad Ave., off Rte. 1, York Beach, 207/363-4911 or 800/456-4911, www.yorkzoo. com). It's not what you'd call a state-of-the-art zoo, but it keeps the kids entertained. Elephant shows and other animal "events" occur three times daily in July-August. Between the zoo and the amusement-park rides, it's easy to spend a day here. Admission (covering the zoo and some of the rides) is in the neighborhood of $21 adults, $16 ages 4-12, $5 under age 4; an unlimited-rides day pass is $11. Zoo-only admission is $15 adults, $9 ages 4-12, $1 under age 4. The zoo is open 10am-5pm Monday-Friday late May-June and September, 10am-5pm Monday-Friday and 10am-6pm Saturday-Sunday July-August; amusement-park hours are noon-9:30pm daily late June-late August, with reduced hours spring and fall.

ENTERTAINMENT AND EVENTS
Live Music

Inn on the Blues (7 Ocean Ave., York Beach,

© HILARY NANGLE

Cape Neddick Light Station, known as "The Nubble," is an icon on Maine's coastline.

207/351-3221, www.innontheblues.com) has live music or a DJ (acoustic, blues, reggae) every night during the summer. The **Ship's Cellar Pub** (480 York St., York Harbor, 800/343-3869) in the York Harbor Inn frequently has live entertainment too. Free concerts are often held at the **Ellis Park Gazebo,** by Short Sands Beach, usually 7pm-9pm early July-early September; check local papers for schedule.

Festivals and Events

Each year, the Old York Historical Society invites decorators to transform a local house for the **Decorator Show House,** culminating in an open house mid-July-mid-August.

Late July-early August, the **York Days** festivities enliven the town with concerts, a road race, sand-castle contests, crafts shows, and fireworks.

York Village's **Annual Harvestfest,** in October, includes entertainment, crafts, hayrides, entertainment, and food.

The annual **Lighting of the Nubble** in late November includes cookies, hot chocolate, music, and an appearance by Santa Claus. The best part, though, is seeing the lighthouse glowing for the holidays.

RECREATION
Walks

Next to Harbor Beach, near the Stage Neck Inn, a sign marks the beginning of the **Cliff Path,** a walkway worth taking for its dramatic harbor views in the shadow of elegant summer cottages. On the one-hour round-trip, you'll pass the York Harbor Reading Room, an exclusive club. The path is on private property, traditionally open to the public courtesy of the owners, but controversy surfaces periodically about property rights, vandalism, and the condition of some sections of the walk. Note that it's called the Cliff Path for a reason: it's not a good choice for little ones.

A less strenuous route is known

variously as the **Shore Path, Harbor Walk,** or **Fisherman's Walk,** running west along the harbor and river from Stage Neck Road and passing the Sayward-Wheeler House before crossing the tiny green-painted Wiggly Bridge leading into the **Steedman Woods** preserve. Carry binoculars for good boat-watching and birding in the 16-acre preserve, owned by the Old York Historical Society. A one-mile double-loop trail takes less than an hour of easy strolling.

Mount Agamenticus

Drive to the summit of Mount Agamenticus ("The Big A") and you're at York County's highest point. It's only 692 feet, but on a clear day you'll have panoramic views of ocean, lakes, woods, and sometimes the White Mountains. The 10,000-acre preserve (www.agamenticus. org), one of the largest remaining expanses of undeveloped forest in coastal New England, is considered among the most biologically diverse wildernesses in Maine. It includes vernal pools and ponds and is home to rare and endangered species. At the summit are a billboard map of the 40-mile trail network and a curious memorial to Saint Aspinquid, a 17th-century Algonquian Indian leader. Mountain biking is also hugely popular on Agamenticus. Take a picnic, a kite, and binoculars. In the fall, if the wind is from the northwest, watch for migrating hawks; in winter, bring a sled for the best downhill run in southern Maine. From Route 1 in Cape Neddick, take Mountain Road (also called Agamenticus Road) 4.2 miles west to the access road.

Golf

The **Ledges Golf Club** (1 Ledges Dr., off Rte. 91, York, 207/351-9999, www.ledgesgolf.com) is an 18-hole course with daily public tee times.

Swimming

Sunbathing and swimming are big draws in York, with four beaches of varying sizes and accessibility. Bear in mind that traffic can be gridlocked along the beachfront (Rte. 1A) in midsummer, so it may take longer than you expect to get anywhere. **Lifeguards** are usually on duty 9:30am-4pm mid-June-Labor Day at Short Sands Beach, Long Sands Beach, and Harbor Beach. Bathhouses at Long Sands and Short Sands are open 9am-7pm daily in midsummer. The biggest parking area (metered) is at Long Sands, but that 1.5-mile beach also draws the most visitors. The scarcest parking is at Harbor Beach near the Stage Neck Inn and at Cape Neddick (Passaconaway) Beach near the Ogunquit town line.

Sea Kayaking

Kayak rentals begin at $55 per day single, $75 double, from **Excursions: Coastal Maine Outfitting Company** (1740 Rte. 1, Cape Neddick, 207/363-0181, www.excursionsin-maine.com). Or sign up for a half-day tour ($60 ages 14 and older, $50 children). A four-hour basics clinic for ages 16 and older is $85. Excursions is based at Dixon's Campground on Route 1, four miles north of the I-95 York exit. **Harbor Adventures** (Harris Island Rd., York Harbor, 207/363-8466, www.harboradventures.com) offers instruction and guided sea-kayaking trips from Kittery through Kennebunkport. Prices begin around $45 for a two-hour harbor tour.

Surfing

Want to catch a wave? For surfing or paddleboard information, lessons, or rentals, call **Liquid Dreams Surf Shop** (171 Long Beach Ave., York, 207/351-2545, www.liquiddreams-surf.com, 10am-6pm daily). It's right across from Long Sands Beach.

Bicycling

The **Daily Spin** (Rte. 1A, York Beach, 207/363-5040) rents beach-cruiser bicycles ($10 per hour, $20 full day). It's at the Daily Grind coffee shop near the zoo.

Fishing

A local expert on fly-fishing, spin fishing, and conventional tackle is **Eldredge Bros. Guide Service** (1480 Rte. 1, Cape Neddick, 207/373-9269, www.eldredgeflyshop.com). Four-hour guided trips for one or two anglers begin at $250 in freshwater, $350 in saltwater.

ACCOMMODATIONS
York Harbor
BED-AND-BREAKFASTS

Bill and Bonnie Alstrom, former innkeepers at Tanglewood Hall, weren't looking to downsize, but on a lark they stumbled upon this woodland cottage, and they were smitten. After more than a year of renovations, they opened ◖ **Morning Glory Inn** (120 Seabury Rd., York Harbor, 207/363-2062, www.morninggloryinnmaine.com, $175-235). A boutique bed-and-breakfast catering to romantics, the Morning Glory has just three guest rooms, all very spacious and private and all with doors to private patios or yards, air-conditioning, TVs with DVD players, fridges, Wi-Fi, and plentiful other little amenities. The living room, in the original section of the house, was a 17th-century cottage, barged over from the Isles of Shoals; the newer post-and-beam great room doubles as a dining area, where a hot breakfast buffet is served. The property is ultraquiet—listen to the birds singing in the gardens; it's truly a magical setting, far removed yet convenient to everything York offers.

FULL-SERVICE INNS

York Harbor Inn (Rte. 1A, York Harbor, 207/363-5119 or 800/343-3869, www.yorkharborinn.com, $179-349 d) is an accommodating spot with a country-inn flavor and a wide variety of guest-room and package-plan options throughout the year. The oldest section of the inn is a 17th-century cabin from the Isles of Shoals. Accommodations are spread out in the inn, the adjacent Yorkshire House, and four elegantly restored houses, all with resident innkeepers: Harbor Hill and Harbor Cliffs are within steps, and the pet-friendly 1730 Harbor Crest and the Chapman Cottage are about a half mile away. All have TVs, phones, free Wi-Fi, and air-conditioning; some have four-poster beds, fireplaces, and whirlpools; many have water views. Rates include a generous continental breakfast.

You can't miss the **Stage Neck Inn** (100 Stage Neck Rd., York Harbor, 207/363-3850 or 800/340-9901, www.stageneck.com, year-round, $315-450), occupying its own private peninsula overlooking York Harbor. Modern resort-style facilities include an indoor and an outdoor pool, tennis courts, golf privileges, a spa, a fitness center, and spectacular views from balconies and terraces. The formal Harbor Porches restaurant (no jeans, entrées $26-30) and the casual Sandpiper Bar and Grille are open to nonguests.

York Beach
HOTEL

For more than 150 years, **The Union Bluff** (8 Beach St., York Beach, 207/363-1333 or 800/833-0721, www.unionbluff.com, $179-399) has stood sentry like a fortress overlooking Short Sands Beach. Guest rooms are split between three buildings, all within spitting distance of the beach. Most have ocean views. All have TVs, air-conditioning, and phones; some have fireplaces, whirlpool baths, or ocean-view decks. Also on the premises are the Beach Street Grill dining room and a pub serving lighter fare. The best deals are the packages, which include breakfast and dinner. The hotel and pub are open year-round; the restaurant is seasonal. It's probably best to avoid dates when there's a wedding in-house.

BED-AND-BREAKFASTS

Everything's casual and flowers are everywhere at the brightly painted **Katahdin Inn** (11 Ocean Ave., York Beach, 207/363-1824, www.thekatahdininn.com, year-round, $95-145), overlooking the breakers of Short Sands Beach. Longtime owners Rae and Paul LeBlanc appropriately refer to it as a "bed and beach." It was built in 1863 and has always been a guesthouse. Nine smallish guest rooms on three floors, eight of them with water views, have four-poster beds and mostly shared baths. Breakfast is not included, but coffee is always available, the rooms have refrigerators, and several eateries are nearby.

Families and vegetarians, you've found your happy place. Not oceanfront but offering ocean views from many rooms and just a short walk from Short Sands Beach is Barbara and Michael Sheff's **Candleshop Inn** (44 Freeman St., York Beach, 207/363-4087 or 888/363-4087, www.candleshopinn.com, $125-195). The 10 guest rooms with private and shared baths are decorated in country cottage style, with area rugs, painted furniture, and florals; many are set up for families. The day begins with a full vegetarian breakfast. Borrow a yoga mat and take it to the inn's Japanese Meditation Garden.

CONDOMINIUM SUITES

Fabulously sited on the oceanfront and overlooking the Nubble Light, the high-end **ViewPoint** (229 Nubble Rd., York Beach, 207/363-2661 or 888/363-4087, www.viewpointhotel.com, $305 one-bedroom-$635 three-bedroom, $1,975-3,845 per week) comprises luxuriously appointed 1-3-bedroom suites. All have gas fireplaces; fully equipped kitchens; washer-dryers; TVs; phones; private patios, porches, or decks; and Wi-Fi. On the premises are an outdoor heated pool, a grilling area, gardens, and a playground.

Cape Neddick

CAMPING

Dixon's Coastal Maine Campground (1740 Rte. 1, Cape Neddick, 207/363-3626, www.dixonscampground.com, $34-40) has more than 100 well-spaced sites on 26 wooded and open acres. It can accommodate tents and small RVs. Electric and water hookups are available. Facilities include a playground and a good-size outdoor heated pool. It's also the base for Excursions sea kayaking.

FOOD

Days and hours of operation reflect peak season and are subject to change.

Local Flavors

Both *Gourmet* and *Saveur* magazines know where to get dogs here. Sometimes the line runs right out the door of the low-ceilinged, reddish-brown roadside shack that houses local institution **Flo's Steamed Dogs** (Rte. 1, opposite the Mountain Rd. turnoff, Cape Neddick, no phone, www.floshotdogs.com). Founder Flo Stacy died in 2000 at age 92, but her legend and her family live on. There is no menu—just steamed Schultz wieners, buns, chips, beverages, and an attitude. The secret? The spicy, sweet-sour hot-dog sauce, allegedly once sought by the H. J. Heinz corporation, but the Stacy family isn't telling or selling. The cognoscenti know to order their dogs only with mayonnaise and the special sauce, nothing heretical such as ketchup or mustard. It's open 11am-3pm, and not a minute later, Thursday-Tuesday year-round.

See those people with their faces pressed to the glass? They're all watching the taffy makers inside **The Goldenrod** (2 Railroad Ave., York Beach, 207/363-2621, www.thegoldenrod.com, 11am-8pm), where machines spew out 180 Goldenrod Kisses a minute, 65 tons a year, and have been at it since 1896. The Goldenrod is an old-fashioned place with a tearoom, a gift shop, an old-fashioned soda fountain with 135 ice cream flavors, and a rustic dining room as well as equally old-fashioned prices.

After viewing The Nubble, head across the road to **Brown's Ice Cream** (232 Nubble Rd., York Beach, 207/363-1277), where unusual flavors complement the standards.

Prepared foods are sold by the pound at **Lucia's Kitchen** (1151 Rte. 1, Cape Neddick, 207/363-5557, www.luciaskitchen.com, 11am-7pm Mon.-Sat.) but sandwiches, cookies, and burritos are always available too. Chef/owner Lucia Velasco-Evans was born in Mexico. In 1995, she won a James Beard award for Best Pastry Chef in the Northeast. Gluten-free and vegetarian choices are available.

Craving jerk chicken or curried goat? Stop by **Jamaican Jerk Center** (1400 Rte. 1, Cape Neddick, 207/351-3033, www.jamaicanjerkcenter.com, 11am-9pm daily), a seasonal take-out with tables under a tent and on the lawn. There's live reggae music on weekends beginning at 4pm.

Stop in at the **Gateway Farmers Market** (Greater York Region Chamber of Commerce Visitors Center, Rte. 1, York, www.gatewaytomaine.org, 9am-1pm Sat. mid-June-early Oct. and Thurs. July and Aug.) and stock up for a picnic. If you still need more, head next door to Stonewall Kitchen.

Family Favorites

The York Harbor Inn's **Ship's Cellar Pub** (11:30am-11:30pm Mon.-Thurs., 11:30am-midnight Fri.-Sat., 3pm-11:30pm Sun.) attracts even the locals. The menu is the same as in the main dining room (burgers to lobster, $8-32), but the setting is far more casual. The space is designed to resemble the interior of a yacht. The pub doubles as a favorite local watering hole, with live music Wednesday-Sunday. Happy hour, with free munchies, is 4pm-6pm weekdays and sometimes draws a raucous crowd.

Wild Willy's (765 Rte. 1, York, 207/363-9924, www.wildwillysburgers.com, 11am-8pm Mon.-Sat., $6-8) has turned burgers into an art form. More than a dozen hefty mouthwatering burgers, all made from certified Angus or natural (chem-free) beef or bison, are available, from the classic Willy burger to the Rio Grande, with roasted green chilies from New Mexico and cheddar cheese. Don't miss the hand-cut fries. Order at the counter before grabbing a seat in the dining area or out on the back deck; the servers will find you when it's ready.

Locals swear by **Rick's All Seasons Café** (240 York St., York, 207/363-5584, 6am-2pm Tues.-Sun.), where the prices are low, the food is good, and the gossip is even better. Have patience: Almost everything is cooked to order.

Casual Dining

It's hard to know whether *Food* or *Shopping* is the right category for **Stonewall Kitchen** (Stonewall Lane, York, 207/351-2712 or 800/207-5267, www.stonewallkitchen.com), a phenomenally successful company that concocts imaginative condiments and other food products, many of which have received national awards. The headquarters building, home to a handsome shop with tasting areas and a "viewing gallery" where you can watch it all happen, is next to the Greater York Region Chamber of Commerce building on Route 1. Go hungry: An espresso bar and an excellent café are on the premises. Stonewall is open daily for breakfast and lunch and light fare in the late afternoon.

"Food that loves you back" is the slogan for **◖ Frankie and Johnny's Natural Foods** (1594 Rte. 1 N., Cape Neddick, 207/363-1909, www.frankie-johnnys.com, from 5pm Wed.-Sun. Feb.-Dec., $23-36). Inside the shingled restaurant, wood floors and pine-colored walls provide the background for the vibrant, internationally seasoned fare of chef John Shaw, who trained at the Culinary Institute of America. Vegetarian and vegan choices are always on the menu, along with fish, seafood, and chicken options, and many dishes can be modified for the gluten-sensitive. Portions are huge, breads and pastas are made in house, and everything is cooked to order, so plan on a leisurely meal. All entrées come with a soup or salad (opt for the house salad—it's gorgeous). Plan on leftovers. Bring your own booze, but leave the credit cards behind, since "plastic is not natural."

Lobster

Friends praise the lobster roll from **The Maine Lobster Outlet** (360 Rte. 1, York, 207/363-9899, www.mainelobsteroutlet.com, 10am-5pm daily, later in summer) as one of the state's best, and say the clam chowder is excellent. It's takeout only.

Grab an oceanfront seat at **Lobster Cove** (756 York St., York Beach, 207/351-1100, from 8:30am daily year-round) and watch the waves roll into Long Sands Beach while enjoying lobster or fried seafood.

INFORMATION AND SERVICES

The Maine Tourism Association operates a **Maine State Visitor Information Center** (1 Rte. 95, Kittery, 207/439-1319) in Kittery between Route 1 and I-95, with access from either road. It's chock-full of brochures and has restrooms and a picnic area.

For York-area information, head for the shingle-style palace of the **Greater York Region Chamber of Commerce** (1 Stonewall Lane, off Rte. 1, York, 207/363-4422, www.gatewaytomaine.org), at I-95's York exit. Inside are restrooms. It's open daily in summer.

GETTING THERE AND AROUND

York is about eight miles or 15 minutes via I-95/The Maine Turnpike; allow at least 20 minutes via Route 1, from Kittery. It's about seven miles or 15 minutes via Route 1 to Ogunquit, but allow more time in summer.

The Maine Turnpike, a toll road, is generally the fastest route if you're trying to get between two towns. Route 1 parallels the turnpike on the ocean side. It's mostly two lanes and is lined with shops, restaurants, motels, and other visitor-oriented sites, which means stop-and-go traffic that often slows to a crawl. If you're traveling locally, it's best to walk or use the local trolley systems, which have the bonus of saving you the agony of finding a parking spot.

The **York Trolley** (207/748-3030, www.yorktrolley.com) operates a **York Beach Shuttle** late June-early September. The service between Long and Short Sands Beaches ($1.50 one-way) runs every 30 minutes 10am-10:15pm.

The **Shore Road Shuttle** (207/324-5762, www.shorelineexplorer.com) operates hourly between York's Short Sands Beach and Ogunquit's Perkins Cove late June-Labor Day; check for an exact schedule; $1 each way; $3 day pass, $10 for 12-ride pass; age 18 and younger ride free.

Ogunquit and Wells

Ogunquit (pop. 892) has been a holiday destination since the indigenous residents named it "beautiful place by the sea." What's the appeal? An unparalleled, unspoiled beach, several top-flight albeit pricey restaurants, a dozen art galleries, and a respected art museum with a view second to none. The town has been home to an art colony attracting the glitterati of the painting world starting with Charles Woodbury in the late 1880s. The summertime crowds continue, multiplying the minuscule year-round population. These days it's an especially gay-friendly community too. Besides the beach, the most powerful magnet is Perkins Cove, a working fishing enclave that looks more like a movie set. The best way to approach the cove is via trolley-bus or on foot, along the shoreline Marginal Way from downtown Ogunquit; midsummer parking in the cove is madness.

Wells (pop. 9,589), once the parent of Ogunquit and since 1980 its immediate neighbor to the north, was settled in 1640. Nowadays it's best known as a long, skinny, family-oriented community with seven miles of splendid beachfront and lots of antiques and used-book shops strewn along Route 1. It also claims two spectacular nature preserves worth a drive from anywhere. At the southern end of Wells, abutting Ogunquit, is **Moody,** an enclave named after 18th-century settler Samuel Moody.

SIGHTS
◖ Ogunquit Museum of American Art (OMAA)

Not many museums can boast a view as stunning as the one at the Ogunquit Museum of American Art (543 Shore Rd., Ogunquit, 207/646-4909, www.ogunquitmuseum.org, 10am-5pm Mon.-Sat., 1pm-5pm Sun. late May-Oct. 31, $10 adults, $9 seniors and students,

free under age 12), nor can many communities boast such renown as a summer art colony. Overlooking Narrow Cove 1.4 miles south of downtown Ogunquit, the museum prides itself on its distinguished permanent 1,600-piece American art collection. Works by Marsden Hartley, Rockwell Kent, Walt Kuhn, Henry Strater, and Thomas Hart Benton, among others, are displayed in five galleries. Special exhibits are mounted each summer, when there is an extensive series of lectures, concerts, and other programs, including the annual "Almost Labor Day Auction," a social season must. OMAA has a well-stocked gift shop, wheelchair access, and landscaped grounds with sculptures, a pond, and manicured lawns.

◖ Marginal Way
No visit to Ogunquit is complete without a leisurely stroll along the Marginal Way, the mile-long foot path edging the ocean from Shore Road (by the Sparhawk Resort) to Perkins Cove. It has been a must-walk since Josiah Chase gave the right-of-way to the town in the 1920s. The best times to appreciate this shrub-lined shorefront walkway are early morning or when everyone's at the beach. En route are tidepools, intriguing rock formations, crashing surf, pocket beaches, benches (although the walk's a cinch and is even partially wheelchair-accessible), and a marker listing the day's high and low tides. When the surf's up, keep a close eye on the kids—the sea has no mercy. A midpoint access is at Israel's Head (behind a sewage plant masquerading as a tiny lighthouse), but getting a parking space is pure luck.

Perkins Cove
Turn-of-the-20th-century photos show Ogunquit's Perkins Cove lined with gray-shingled shacks used by a hardy colony of

No visit to Ogunquit is complete without walking the Marginal Way.

© HILARY NANGLE

local fishermen, fellows who headed offshore to make a tough living in little boats. They'd hardly recognize it today. Although the cove remains a working lobster-fishing harbor, several old shacks have been reincarnated as boutiques and restaurants, and photographers go crazy shooting the quaint inlet spanned by a little pedestrian drawbridge. In the cove are galleries, gift shops, a range of eateries (fast food to lobster to high-end dining), boat excursions, and public restrooms.

◖ Wells Reserve at Laudholm Farm

Known locally as Laudholm Farm (the name of the restored 19th-century visitors center), Wells National Estuarine Research Reserve (342 Laudholm Farm Rd., Wells, 207/646-1555) occupies 1,690 acres of woods, beach, and coastal salt marsh on the southern boundary of the Rachel Carson National Wildlife Refuge, just

0.5 mile east of Route 1. Seven miles of trails wind through the property. The best trail is the Salt Marsh Loop, with a boardwalk section leading to an overlook with panoramic views of the marsh and Little River inlet. Another winner is the Barrier Beach Walk, a 1.3-mile round-trip that goes through multiple habitats all the way to beautiful Laudholm Beach. Allow 1.5 hours for either; you can combine the two. Some trails are wheelchair-accessible. The informative exhibits in the visitors center (10am-4pm Mon.-Sat., noon-4pm Sun. late May-mid-Oct., 10am-4pm Mon.-Fri. Oct.-Mar., closed mid-Dec.-mid-Jan.) make a valuable prelude for enjoying the reserve. An extensive program schedule (Apr.-Nov.) includes lectures, nature walks, and children's programs. Reservations are required for some programs. Trails are accessible 7am-dusk. Late May-mid-October, admission is charged: $4 adults, $1 ages 6-16, maximum $10 per car.

Rachel Carson National Wildlife Refuge

Eleven chunks of coastal Maine real estate between Kittery Point and Cape Elizabeth make up this refuge (321 Port Rd./Rte. 9, Wells, 207/646-9226, http://rachelcarson.fws.gov) headquartered at the northern edge of Wells near the Kennebunkport town line. Pick up a *Carson Trail Guide* at the refuge office (parking is very limited) and follow the mile-long wheelchair-accessible walkway past tidal creeks, salt pans, and salt marshes. It's a bird-watcher's paradise during migration seasons. Office hours are 8am-4:30pm Monday-Friday year-round; trail access is sunrise-sunset daily year-round. Leashed pets are allowed.

Ogunquit Arts Collaborative Gallery

Closer to downtown Ogunquit is the Ogunquit Arts Collaborative Gallery (Shore Rd. and Bourne Lane, Ogunquit, 207/646-8400, www.barngallery.org, 11am-5pm Mon.-Sat., 1pm-5pm Sun. late May-early Oct., free), also known as the Barn Gallery, featuring the works of member artists, an impressive group. The OAC is the showcase for the Ogunquit Art Association, established by Charles Woodbury, who was inspired to open an art school in Perkins Cove in the late 19th century. Special programs throughout the season include concerts, workshops, gallery talks, and an art auction.

Wells Auto Museum

The late Glenn Gould's collection of more than 80 vintage vehicles, some restored, others not, plus a collection of old-fashioned nickelodeons (bring nickels and dimes; they work), are jam-packed into the Wells Auto Museum (Rte. 1, Wells, 207/646-9064, www.wellsautomuseum.com, 10am-5pm daily late June-late Sept., $7 adults, $4 ages 6-12). From the outside it looks like a big warehouse; inside its treasures include an original 1918 Stutz Bearcat, four Pierce Arrows, a Stanley Steamer, and an emphasis on Brass Era vehicles.

Local History Museum

Ogunquit's history is preserved in the **Ogunquit Heritage Museum** (86 Obeds Lane, Dorothea Jacobs Grant Common, Ogunquit, 207/646-0296, www.ogunquitheritagemuseum.org, 1pm-5pm Tues.-Sat. June-Sept., donation), which opened in 2001 in the restored Captain James Winn House, a 1785 cape house listed on the National Register of Historic Places. Exhibits here and in a new ell focus on Ogunquit's role as an art colony, its maritime heritage, town history, and local architecture.

ENTERTAINMENT
Ogunquit Playhouse

Having showcased top-notch professional theater since the 1930s, the 750-seat Ogunquit Playhouse (Rte. 1, Ogunquit, 207/646-5511, www.ogunquitplayhouse.org), a summer classic, knows how to do it right: It presents comedies and musicals, late May-late Oct. with big-name stars. The air-conditioned building is wheelchair accessible. The box office is open daily in season, beginning in early May; tickets range $39-74. The playhouse also presents a children's series. Parking can be a hassle; consider walking the short distance from the Bourne Lane trolley-bus stop.

Live Music

Ogunquit has several nightspots with good reputations for food and live entertainment. Best known is **Jonathan's** (2 Bourne Lane, Ogunquit, 207/646-4777 or 800/464-9934 in Maine), where national headliners often are on the schedule upstairs. Advance tickets are cheaper than at the door, and dinner guests (entrées $23-34) get preference for seats; all show seats are reserved.

Ogunquit Performing Arts (207/646-6170,

© TOM NANGLE

The Ogunquit Playhouse has showcased top-notch professional entertainment since the 1930s.

www.ogunquitperformingarts.org) presents a full slate of programs, including classical concerts, ballet, and theater. The **Wells Summer Concert Series** runs most Saturday evenings early July-early September at the Hope Hobbs Gazebo in Wells Harbor Park. A wide variety of music is represented, from sing-alongs to swing.

FESTIVALS AND EVENTS

During **Restaurant Week** in early June, Ogunquit-area restaurants offer specials.

Harbor Fest takes place in July in Harbor Park in Wells and includes a concert, a crafts fair, a parade, a chicken barbecue, and children's activities.

In August Ogunquit hosts the annual **Sidewalk Art Show and Sale.**

Capriccio is a performing arts festival in Oguquit with daytime and evening events held during the first week of September. The second weekend that month, the Wells National

Estuarine Research Reserve (Laudholm Farm) hosts the **Laudholm Nature Crafts Festival,** a two-day juried crafts fair with children's activities and guided nature walks.

SHOPPING

Antiques are a Wells specialty. You'll find more than 50 shops with a huge range of prices. The majority are on Route 1. **R. Jorgensen Antiques** (502 Post Rd./Rte. 1, Wells, 207/646-9444) is a phenomenon in itself, filling 11 showrooms in two buildings with European and American 18th- and 19th-century furniture and accessories. **MacDougall-Gionet Antiques and Associates** (2104 Post Rd./Rte. 1, Wells, 207/646-3531) has been in business since 1959, and its reputation is stellar. The 65-dealer shop, in an 18th-century barn, carries American and European country and formal furniture and accessories.

If you've been scouring antiquarian

bookshops for a long-wanted title, chances are you'll find it at **Douglas N. Harding Rare Books** (2152 Post Rd./Rte. 1, Wells, 207/646-8785 or 800/228-1398). Well cataloged and organized, the sprawling bookshop at any given time stocks upward of 100,000 books, prints, and maps, plus a hefty selection of Maine and New England histories.

Fans of fine craft, especially contemporary art glass, shouldn't miss **Panache** (307 Main St., Ogunquit, 207/646-4878).

RECREATION
Water Sports
BEACHES

One of Maine's most scenic and unspoiled sandy beachfronts, Ogunquit's 3.5-mile stretch of sand fringed with sea grass is a magnet for hordes of sunbathers, spectators, swimmers, surfers, and sand-castle builders. Getting there means crossing the Ogunquit

River via one of three access points. For Ogunquit's **Main Beach**—with a bathhouse and big crowds—take Beach Street. To reach **Footbridge Beach,** marginally less crowded, either take Ocean Street and the footbridge or take Bourne Avenue to Ocean Avenue in adjacent Wells and walk back toward Ogunquit. **Moody Beach,** at Wells's southern end, is technically private property, a subject of considerable legal dispute. Lifeguards are on duty all summer at the public beaches, and there are restrooms in all three areas. The beach is free, but parking is not. Rates range $15-25 per day and lots fill up early on warm mid-summer days. After 3:30pm some parking is free. It's far more sensible to opt for the frequent trolley-buses.

Wells beaches continue where Ogunquit's leave off. **Crescent Beach** (Webhannet Dr. between Eldredge Rd. and Mile Rd.) is the tiniest, with tidepools, no facilities, and

© HILARY NANGLE

Ogunquit's 3.5-mile stretch of sand is a magnet for beach lovers.

limited parking. **Wells Beach** (Mile Rd. to Atlantic Ave.) is the major (and most crowded) beach, with lifeguards, restrooms, and parking. Around the other side of Wells Harbor is **Drakes Island Beach** (take Drakes Island Rd. at the blinking light), a less crowded spot with restrooms and lifeguards. Walk northeast from Drakes Island Beach and you'll eventually reach Laudholm Beach, with great birding along the way. Summer beach-parking fees (pay-and-display) are $16 per day/$8 afternoon for nonresidents ($5 for a motorcycle, $25 for an RV); if you're staying longer, a 10-token pass ($75) is a better bargain.

BOAT EXCURSIONS

Depending on your interests, you can go deep-sea fishing, whale-watching, or just gawking out of Perkins Cove in Ogunquit.

Between April and early November, Captain Tim Tower runs half-day (departing 4pm, $50 pp) and full-day (departing 7am, $85 pp) **deep-sea fishing trips** aboard the 40-foot *Bunny Clark* (207/646-2214, www. bunnyclark.com), moored in Perkins Cove. Reservations are necessary. Tim has a science degree, so he's a wealth of marine biology information. All gear is provided, and the crew will fillet your catch for you; dress warmly and wear sunblock.

Barnacle Billy's Dock at Perkins Cove is home port for the Hubbard family's **Finestkind Cruises** (207/646-5227, www.finestkind-cruises.com). Motorboat options consist of 1.5-hour, 14-mile Nubble Lighthouse cruises; one-hour cocktail cruises; a 75-minute breakfast cruise, complete with coffee, juice, and a muffin; and 50-minute lobster-boat trips. Rates run $16-24 adults, $8-12 children. Also available are 1.75-hour sails ($30 pp) aboard *The Cricket,* a locally built wooden sailboat. Reservations are advisable but usually unnecessary midweek. Finestkind does not accept credit cards.

EQUIPMENT RENTALS

At **Wheels and Waves** (579 Post Rd./Rte. 1, Wells, 207/646-5774, www.wheelsnwaves. com), bike or surfboard rentals are $25 per day, including delivery to some hotels; a stand-up paddleboard is $20, a single kayak is $55, and a double is $65.

Put in right at the harbor and explore the estuary from **Webhannet River Kayak and Canoe Rentals** (345 Harbor Rd., Wells, 207/646-9649, www.webhannetriver.com). Rates begin at $25 solo, $40 tandem for two hours.

Golf

The 18-hole Donald Ross-designed **Cape Neddick Country Club** (650 Shore Rd., 207/361-2011, www.capeneddickgolf.com) is a semiprivate 18-hole course with a restaurant and a driving range.

ACCOMMODATIONS

Rates are for peak season; most charge less in spring and fall. Most properties are open only seasonally.

Ogunquit
MOTELS

You're almost within spitting distance of Perkins Cove at the 37-room **Riverside Motel** (159 Shore Rd., 207/646-2741, www.riverside-motel.com, $199-249), where you can perch on your balcony and watch the action or, for that matter, join it. Guest rooms have phones, air-conditioning, refrigerators, Wi-Fi, cable TV, and fabulous views. Rates include continental breakfast. The entire 3.5-acre property is smoke-free.

Juniper Hill Inn (336 Main St., 207/646-4501 or 800/646-4544, www.ogunquit.com, year-round, $149-254) is a well-run motel-style lodging on five acres close to downtown Ogunquit, with a footpath to the beach. Amenities include refrigerators, cable TV, coin-operated laundry, a fitness center, indoor and outdoor pools and hot tubs, and golf privileges. Rooms have all the amenities, including free Wi-Fi.

The frills are few, but the **Towne Lyne Motel** (747 Main St./Rte. 1, 207/646-2955, www. townelynemotel.com, $139-179) is a charmer set back from the highway amid manicured lawns. Rooms are air-conditioned and have free Wi-Fi and phone, refrigerators, and microwaves; some have screened porches. Request a riverside room.

COTTAGES

It's nearly impossible to land a peak-season cottage at **The Dunes** (518 Main St., 207/646-2612, www.dunesonthewaterfront.com), but it's worth trying. The property is under its third generation of ownership, and guests practically will their weeks to their descendants. Nineteen tidy, well-equipped 1-2-bedroom housekeeping

cottages with screened porches and wood-burning fireplaces as well as 17 guest rooms are generously spaced on shady, grassy lawns that roll down to the river, with the dunes just beyond. Facilities include a dock with rowboats, a pool, and lawn games. Amenities include Wi-Fi, TVs, phones, and refrigerators. It's all meticulously maintained. In peak season, the 1-2-bedroom cottages require a 1-2-week minimum stay; guest rooms require three nights. Nightly rates begin around $150 for rooms, $250 for cottages.

ECLECTIC PROPERTIES

◖ **The Beachmere Inn** (62 Beachmere Pl., 207/646-2021 or 800/336-3983, www.beachmereinn.com, year-round, $170-440) occupies an enviable oceanfront location on the Marginal Way, yet is just steps from downtown. The private family-owned and operated property comprises an updated Victorian inn,

© HILARY NANGLE

The Beachmere Inn has a prime location overlooking Ogunquit Beach on Marginal Way.

a new seaside motel, and other buildings, all meticulously maintained and often updated. It even has pocket beaches. All rooms have air-conditioning, TVs, phones, and kitchenettes; most have balconies, decks, or terraces; some have fireplaces; almost all have jaw-dropping ocean views. There's also a small spa with a hot tub, steam sauna, and fitness room; and a pub serving light fare and drinks. Morning coffee and pastries are provided.

It's not easy to describe the **Sparhawk Oceanfront Resort** (41 Shore Rd., 207/646-5562, www.thesparhawk.com, $200-320), a sprawling one-of-a-kind place popular with honeymooners, sedate families, and seniors. There's lots of tradition in this thriving six-acre complex—it has had various incarnations since the turn of the 20th century—and the "Happily Filled" sign regularly hangs out front. Out back is the Atlantic Ocean with forever views, and the Marginal Way starts right here. It offers a tennis court, gardens, and a heated pool; breakfast is included. The 87 guest rooms in four buildings vary from motel-type (best views) rooms and suites to inn-type suites. There's a seven-night minimum during July-August.

BED-AND-BREAKFASTS

When you want to be at the center of the action, book a room at **2 Village Square Inn** (14 Village Square Ln., 207/646-5779, www.2vsquare.com, $149-269). The walk-to-everything location puts the beach, the Marginal Way, shops, restaurants, and more all within footsteps, if you can tear yourself away from the dreamy views, heated outdoor pool, hut tub, and even an on-site massage room. Owners Scott Osgood and Bruce Senecal have earned a reputation as conscientious innkeepers who aim to please. They also operate the **Nellie Littlefield Inn & Spa** (27 Shore Rd., 207/646-1692, www.nliogunquit.com, $229-309), a magnificently restored intown Victorian, and

the **Gazebo Inn** (572 Main St., 207/646-3773, www.gazeboinnogt.com, $149-499), a carefully renovated 1847 farmhouse and barn within walking distance of Footbridge Beach. All serve a full breakfast buffet.

Jacqui Grant's warm welcome, gracious hospitality, and stellar breakfasts combined with a quiet residential location within walking distance of both the village and Footbridge Beach have earned **Almost Home** (27 King's Ln., 207/641-1754, www.almosthomeinnogunquit.com, $185-225) a stellar reputation. She often serves afternoon cheese with wine from her son's California winery. Rooms are spacious and have nice seating areas, and the backyard makes a quiet retreat.

Built in 1899 for a prominent Maine lumbering family, **Rockmere Lodge** (40 Stearns Rd., 207/646-2985, www.rockmere.com, year-round, $190-240) underwent a meticulous six-month restoration in the early 1990s. Near the Marginal Way on a peaceful street, the hand-some home has eight comfortable Victorian guest rooms, all with CD players and cable TV (a massive library of films and CDs is available) and most with ocean views. Rates include a generous breakfast. A wraparound veranda, a gazebo, and "The Lookout," a third-floor windowed nook with comfy chairs, make it easy to settle in and just watch the passersby on the Marginal Way. Beach towels, chairs, and umbrellas are provided for guests. Pets are not allowed; there are dogs in residence.

RESORTS

Founded in 1872, **The Cliff House Resort and Spa** (Shore Rd., 207/361-1000, www.cliffhousemaine.com, late Mar.-early Dec., $275-370), a self-contained complex, sprawls over 70 acres topping the edge of Bald Head Cliff midway between the centers of York and Ogunquit. Fourth-generation innkeeper Kathryn Weare keeps updating and modernizing the facilities. Among the most recent additions is a spa building with oversize rooms with king beds, gas fireplaces, and balconies as well as a full-service spa, an indoor pool, an outdoor infinity pool, and a glass-walled fitness center overlooking the Atlantic. A central check-in building with an indoor amphitheater connects the main building to the spa building. The 150 guest rooms and suites vary widely in decor, from old-fashioned to contemporary; all have cable TV and phones, some have gas fireplaces, and most have a spectacular ocean view. Other facilities include a dining room, a lounge, family indoor and outdoor pools, a games room, and tennis courts. Eight pet-friendly rooms ($25) have a bowl, a bed, and treats, and there's a fenced-in exercise area. Packages offer the best bang for the buck.

Wells

Once part of a giant 19th-century dairy farm, the **Beach Farm Inn** (97 Eldredge Rd., 207/646-8493, www.beachfarminn.com, year-round, $100-150) is a 2.5-acre oasis in a rather congested area 0.2 mile off Route 1. Guests can swim in the pool, relax in the library, or walk 0.25 mile down the road to the beach. Five of the eight guest rooms have private baths (two are detached); third-floor rooms have air-conditioning. Rates include a full breakfast; a cottage rents for $725 per week.

Even closer to the beach is **Haven by the Sea** (59 Church St., Wells Beach, 207/646-4194, www.havenbythesea.com, $239-319), a heavenly bed-and-breakfast in a former church. Innkeepers John and Susan Jarvis have kept the original floor plan, which allows for some surprises. Inside are hardwood floors, cathedral ceilings, and stained-glass windows. The confessional is now a full bar, and the altar has been converted to a dining area that opens to a marsh-view terrace—the bird-watching is superb. Guest rooms have sitting areas, and the suite has a whirlpool tub

and a fireplace. Guests have plenty of room to relax, including a living area with a fireplace. Rates include a full breakfast and afternoon hors d'oeuvres.

FOOD

Days and hours of operation reflect peak season and are subject to change.

Ogunquit
LOCAL FLAVORS
The Egg and I (501 Maine St./Rte. 1, 207/646-8777, www.eggandibreakfast.com, 6am-2pm daily, no credit cards) has more than 200 menu choices and earns high marks for its omelets and waffles. You can't miss it; there's always a crowd. Lunch choices are served after 11am.

Equally popular is **Amore Breakfast** (309 Shore Rd., 207/646-6661, www.amorebreakfast.com, 7am-1pm daily). Choose from 14 omelets, eight versions of eggs Benedict (including lobster and a spirited rancheros version topped with salsa and served with guacamole), as well as French toast, waffles, and all the regulars and irregulars.

Eat in or take out from **Village Food Market** (Main St., Ogunquit Center, 207/646-2122, www.villagefoodmarket.com). A breakfast sandwich is less than $3, subs and sandwiches are available in three sizes, and there's even a children's menu. The Pick Three prepared dinner special includes an entrée and two side dishes for $9.95.

Scrumptious baked goods, tantalizing salads, and vegetarian lunch items are available to go at Mary Breen's fabulous **Bread and Roses** (246 Main St., 207/646-4227, www.breadandrosesbakery.com, 7am-5pm daily), a small bakery right downtown with a few tables outside.

Harbor Candy Shop (26 Main St., 207/646-8078 or 800/331-5856) is packed with the most outrageous chocolate imaginable. Fudge, truffles, and turtles are all made on-site.

ETHNIC FARE

The closest thing to an upscale rustic French country inn is the dining room at **❨ 98 Provence** (262 Shore Rd., 207/646-9898, www.98provence.com, 7am-11am and 5:30pm-close daily), also home to a bakery out back (7am-5pm daily). Chef-owner Pierre Gignac turns out appetizers and superb entrées in the $23-35 range, but there are also three fixed menus ($30-45). Possibilities may include foie gras, escargot, rabbit, and cassoulet, and there's always a fish of the day. Service is attentive and well paced. Don't miss it, and be sure to make reservations. It's also a good choice for breakfast ($6-10) and for nibbles in the lounge.

The best and most authentic Italian dining is at **Angelina's Ristorante** (655 Main St./Rte. 1, 207/646-0445, www.angelinasogunquit.com, 4:30pm-10pm daily year-round, $16-29). Chef-owner David Giarusso uses recipes handed down from his great-grandmother, Angelina Peluso. Dine in the dining room, wine room, lounge, or out on the terrace, choosing from pastas, risottos (the house specialty), and other classics.

Another Italian outpost is **Caffe Prego** (44 Shore Rd., 207/646-7734, www.caffepregoogt.com, 11:30am-9pm daily, $9-22). Owners Donato Tramuto and Jeffrey Porter have created an authentic taste of Tuscany. They've imported Italian equipment and use traditional ingredients to create coffees, pastries, paninis, brick-oven pizzas, pastas, salads, and gelatos, served inside or on the terrace.

CASUAL DINING

Gypsy Sweethearts (10 Shore Rd., 207/646-7021, www.gypsysweethearts.com, from 5:30 daily, entrées $19-32) serves in four rooms on the ground floor of a restored house, on a deck, and in a garden. It's one of the region's most reliable restaurants, and the creative menu is infused with ethnic accents and includes vegetarian choices. Reservations are advised in midsummer.

Mediterranean fare is finessed with a dollop of creativity and a pinch of Maine flavors at **❨ Five-O** (50 Shore Rd., 207/646-6365, www.five-oshoreroad.com, dinner 5pm-10pm daily, brunch 8am-11:30am Sat.-Sun.), one of the region's top restaurants for casual dining. The menus changes frequently, but the housemade pastas and entrées usually run $18-40. Lighter fare ($10-24) is available until 11pm in the lounge, where martinis are a specialty. In the off-season, multicourse regional dinners are held about once a month ($70). Valet parking is available.

Boisterous and lively, **The Front Porch** (9 Shore Rd., 207/646-4005, www.thefrontporch.net, dinner from 4pm Wed.-Sat., from 1pm Sun., $10-29) is not for those looking for romantic dining, but it is a good choice for families with divergent tastes. The menu ranges from flatbread pizzas to rack of lamb.

DINING WITH A VIEW

There's not much between you and Spain when you get a window seat at **MC** (Oarweed Lane, Perkins Cove, 207/646-6263, www.markandclarkrestaurants.com, 11:30am-3:30pm and 5pm-11pm daily late May-mid-Oct., Wed.-Sun. mid-Oct.-Dec. and Feb.-late May, dinner entrées $25-37), sister restaurant of the mega-high-end Arrows Restaurant. Almost every table on both floors has a view. Service is attentive, and the food is tops and in keeping with James Beard Award-winning chefs Mark Gaier and Clark Frasier, ultrafresh. If you can't justify the splurge for Arrows, get a taste of their cuisine here. The bar menu, also served in the dining room by request, is available until 11pm. There's often live music on Wednesday night. A jazz brunch is served beginning at 11am Sunday September-June. Reservations are essential for dinner.

Equally if not more impressive are the views from the dining room at **The Cliff House** (Shore Rd., 207/361-1000, entrées $20-36). Go for the breakfast buffet 7:30am-1pm Sunday. Service can be so-so. Before or after dining, wander the grounds.

DESTINATION DINING

Restrain yourself for a couple of days and then splurge on an elegant dinner at **Arrows** (Berwick Rd., about 1.5 miles west of Rte. 1, 207/361-1100, www.markandclarkrestaurants. com, dinner from 6pm Wed.-Sun. June-mid-Oct.; Thurs.-Sun. late Apr.-May, late Oct., and Dec.; Fri.-Sun. Nov.), one of Maine's finest—and priciest—restaurants. In a beautifully restored 18th-century farmhouse overlooking well-tended gardens (including a one-acre kitchen garden that supplies about 90 percent of the produce), co-owners Mark Gaier and Clark Frasier, the 2010 James Beard Best Chefs Northeast Award winners, do everything right. Plan on spending at least $250 per couple. On Friday nights a set, three-course, bistro menu is offered ($40). A credit card is required for reservations—essential in midsummer and on weekends. Jackets are preferred for men, and shorts are not allowed.

LOBSTER

Creative marketing, a knockout view, and efficient service help explain why more than 1,000 pounds of lobster bite the dust every summer day at **Barnacle Billy's** (Perkins Cove, 207/646-5575 or 800/866-5575, www.barnbilly.com, 11am-9pm daily seasonally). Billy's has a full liquor license; try for the deck, with a front-row seat on Perkins Cove.

Less flashy and less pricey is **The Lobster Shack** (Perkins Cove, 207/646-2941, www. lobster-shack.com, 11am-9pm daily), serving lobsters, stews, chowders, and some landlubber choices too.

Wells

LOCAL FLAVORS

Bean suppers are held 5pm-7pm on the first Saturday of the month May-October at the Masonic Hall on Sanford Road.

For scrumptious baked goods and made-to-order sandwiches, head to **Borealis Bread** (Rte. 1, 8:30am-5:30pm Mon.-Sat., 9am-4pm Sun.), in the Aubuchon Hardware plaza adjacent to the Wells Auto Museum.

Pick up all sorts of fresh goodies at the **Wells Farmers Market** (1pm-5:30pm Wed.) in the Town Hall parking lot (208 Sanford Rd.).

FAMILY FAVORITES

For fresh lobster, lobster rolls, fish-and-chips, chowders, and homemade desserts, you can't go wrong at the Cardinali family's ⟨ **Fisherman's Catch** (Harbor Rd./Rte. 1, 207/646-8780, www.fishermanscatchwells. com, 11:30am-9pm daily early May-mid-Oct., $8-21). Big windows in the rustic dining room frame the marsh; some even have binoculars for wildlife spotting. It might seem out of the way, but trust me, the locals all know this little gem.

A good steak in the land of lobster? You betcha: **The Steakhouse** (1205 Post Rd./Rte. 1, 207/646-4200, www.the-steakhouse.com, 4pm-9:30pm Tues.-Sun., entrées $15-30) is a great big barn of a place where steaks are hand cut from USDA prime and choice corn-fed Western beef that has never been frozen. Chicken, seafood, lobster (great stew), and even a vegetarian stir-fry are also on the menu, and a children's menu is available. Service is efficient, but they don't take reservations, so be prepared for a wait.

FINE DINING

Chef Joshua W. Mather of ⟨ **Joshua's** (1637 Rte. 1, 207/646-3355, www.joshuas.biz, from 5pm daily, entrées $21-35) grew up on his family's nearby organic farm, and produce from that farm highlights the menu. In a true family operation, his parents not only still work the farm, but also work in the restaurant, a converted 1774 home with many of its original architectural elements. Everything is made on the premises, from the fabulous bread to the hand-churned ice cream. The Atlantic haddock, with caramelized onion crust, chive oil, and wild mushroom risotto, is a signature dish, and it alone is worth coming for. A vegetarian pasta entrée is offered nightly. Save room for the maple walnut pie with maple ice cream. Yes, it's gilding the lily, but you can always walk the beach afterward. Reservations are essential for the dining rooms, but the full menu is also served in the bar.

INFORMATION AND SERVICES

At the southern edge of Ogunquit, right next to the Ogunquit Playhouse, the **Ogunquit Chamber of Commerce's Welcome Center** (Rte. 1, Ogunquit, 207/646-2939, www.ogunquit.org) provides all the usual visitor information and has public restrooms. Ask for the Touring and Trolley Route Map, showing the Marginal Way, beach locations, and public restrooms. The chamber of commerce's annual visitor booklet thoughtfully carries a high-tide calendar for the summer.

Just over the Ogunquit border in Wells (actually in Moody) is the **Wells Information Center** (Rte. 1 at Bourne Ave., 207/646-2451, www.wellschamber.org).

The handsome fieldstone **Ogunquit Memorial Library** (74 Shore Rd., Ogunquit,

207/646-9024) is downtown's only building on the National Register of Historic Places. Or visit the **Wells Public Library** (1434 Post Rd./ Rte. 1, 207/646-8181, www.wells.lib.me.us).

GETTING THERE AND AROUND

Ogunquit is about seven miles or 15 minutes via via Route 1, from York. Wells is about six miles or 12 minutes via Route 1 from Ogunquit. From York to Wells, it's about 15.5 miles or 20 minutes on I-95. When traveling in summer, expect heavy traffic and delays on Route 1.

Amtrak's Downeaster (800/872-7245, www.amtrakdowneaster.com), which connects Boston's North Station with Portland, Maine, stops in Wells. The Shoreline Explorer trolley connects in season.

The seasonal **Shoreline Explorer** (207/324-5762, www.shorelineexplorer.com) trolley system makes it possible to connect from York to Kennebunkport without your car. Each town's system is operated separately and has its own fees. The **Shoreline Trolley Line 2/Shore Road Shuttle** ($1 one way, $3 day pass, $10 12-ride multipass, free for kids under 18) operates between Short Sands Beach, in York, and Perkins Cove, Ogunquit; **Shoreline Trolley Route 3/ Ogunquit Trolley** ($1.50 one way, $1 ages 10 and under) connects to **Shoreline Trolley Route 4** ($1 one way, $3 day pass, $10 12-ride multipass, free for kids under 18), which serves Wells and the Wells Transportation Center, where the Amtrak *Downeaster* train stops.

The Kennebunks

The world may have first learned of Kennebunkport when George Herbert Walker Bush was president, but Walkers and Bushes have owned their summer estate here for three generations. Visitors continue to come to the Kennebunks (the collective name for **Kennebunk, Kennebunkport, Cape Porpoise,** and **Goose Rocks Beach**) hoping to catch a glimpse of the former first family, but they also come for the terrific ambience, bed-and-breakfasts, boutiques, boats, biking, and beaches.

The Kennebunks' earliest European settlers arrived in the mid-1600s. By the mid-1700s, shipbuilding had become big business in the area. Two ancient local cemeteries—North Street and Evergreen—provide glimpses of the area's heritage. Its Historic District reveals Kennebunk's moneyed past—the homes where wealthy ship owners and shipbuilders once lived, sending their vessels to the Caribbean and around the globe. Today, unusual shrubs and a dozen varieties of rare maples still line Summer Street—the legacy of ship captains in the global trade. Another legacy is the shiplap construction in many houses—a throwback to a time when labor was cheap and lumber plentiful. Closer to the beach in Lower Village stood the workshops of sailmakers, carpenters, and mast makers whose output drove the booming trade to success.

Although Kennebunkport (pop. 3,474) draws most of the sightseers and summer traffic, Kennebunk (pop. 10,798) feels more like a year-round community. Its old-fashioned downtown has a mix of shops, restaurants, and attractions. Yes, its beaches are also well known, but many visitors drive right through the middle of Kennebunk without stopping to enjoy its assets.

SIGHTS
◖ Seashore Trolley Museum

There's nothing quite like an antique electric trolley to dredge up nostalgia for bygone days. With a collection of more than 250 transit vehicles (more than two dozen trolleys on display), the Seashore Trolley Museum (195 Log Cabin Rd., Kennebunkport, 207/967-2800, www.trolleymuseum.org, $10 adults, $8 seniors, $7.50 ages 6-16) verges on trolley mania. Whistles blowing and bells clanging, restored streetcars do frequent trips (10:05am-4:15pm) on a 3.5-mile loop through the nearby woods. Ride as often as you wish, and then check out the activity in the streetcar workshop and go wild in the trolley-oriented gift shop. Bring a picnic lunch and enjoy it here. Special events are held throughout the summer, including Ice Cream and Sunset Trolley Rides (7pm Wed.-Thurs., July-Aug. $5, includes ice cream). And here's an interesting wrinkle: Make a reservation, plunk down $60, and you can have a one-hour "Motorman" experience driving your own trolley (with help, of course). The museum is 1.7 miles southeast of Route 1. It's open 10am-5pm daily late May-mid-October and on weekends in May, late October, and Christmas Prelude.

Walker's Point: The Bush Estate

There's no public access to Walker's Point, but you can join the sidewalk gawkers on Ocean Avenue overlooking George and Barbara Bush's summer compound. The 41st president and his wife lead a low-key laidback life when they're here, so if you don't spot them through binoculars, you may well run into them at a shop or restaurant in town. Intown Trolley's regular narrated tours go right past the house—or it's an easy, scenic family walk from Kennebunkport's

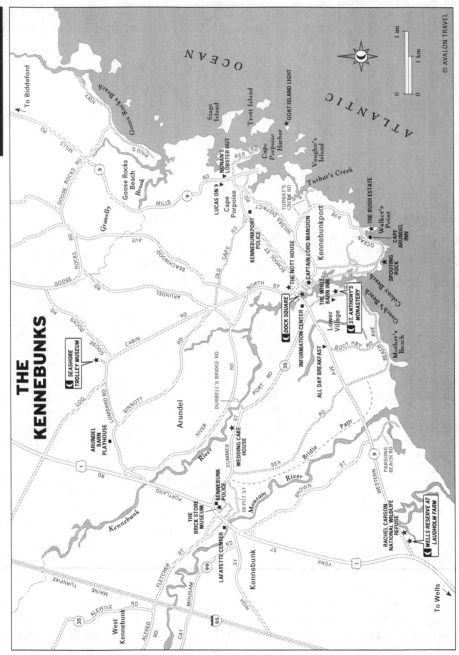

THE KENNEBUNKS

OCEAN

ATLANTIC

© AVALON TRAVEL

To Biddeford

Goose Rocks Beach

MILLS RD

KING'S HWY

GOOSE ROCKS RD

Goose Rocks Beach Brook

Gravelly

GOOSE ROCKS RD

BEACHWOOD RD

MILLS RD

NUNAN'S LOBSTER HUT

Stage Island

Trott Island

GOAT ISLAND LIGHT

Cape Porpoise Harbor

Vaughn's Island

PIER RD

LUCAS ON 9

Cape Porpoise

WILDES DISTRICT RD

OLD CAPE RD

TURBAT'S CREEK RD

Turbat's Creek

THE BUSH ESTATE

Walker's Point

CAPE ARUNDEL INN

OCEAN AVE

KENNEBUNKPORT POLICE

SCHOOL ST

THE NOTT HOUSE

CAPTAIN LORD MANSION

Kennebunkport

SPOUTING ROCK

ARUNDEL RD

NORTH ST

DOCK SQUARE

INFORMATION CENTER

THE WHEEL BARN INN

ST. ANTHONY'S MONASTERY

Lower Village

Colony Beach

Goose's Beach

SEASHORE TROLLEY MUSEUM

GOOSE RD

LOG CABIN RD

SINNOTT RD

DURRELL'S BRIDGE RD

PORT RD

BOOT HBY RD

ALL DAY BREAKFAST

Mother's Beach

BEACH AVE

ARUNDEL BARN PLAYHOUSE

LOMBARD RD

Arundel

Kennebunk River

SUMMER ST

WEDDING CAKE HOUSE

SEA RD

Bridle Path

Mousam River

BROWN ST

PARSONS BEACH RD

WESTERN AVE

PORTLAND RD

THE BRICK STORE MUSEUM

KENNEBUNK POLICE

DEPOT ST

Kennebunk

York ST

RACHEL CARSON NATIONAL WILDLIFE REFUGE

WELLS RESERVE AT LAUDHOLM FARM

MAINE TURNPIKE

West Kennebunk

ALEWIVE RD

ALFRED RD

CAT

MOUSAM RD

FLETCHER ST

LAFAYETTE CENTER

HIGH ST

Kennebunk

To Wells

1 mi

1 km

SOUTHERN COAST

© HILARY NANGLE

Don't miss wandering the oceanfront property of St. Ann's Church in Kennebunkport.

Dock Square. On the way, you'll pass **St. Ann's Church,** whose stones came from the ocean floor, and the paths to **Spouting Rock** and **Blowing Cave,** two natural phenomena that create spectacular water fountains if you manage to be there midway between high and low tides.

Wedding Cake House

The Wedding Cake House (104 Summer St., Kennebunk) is a private residence, so you can't go inside, but it's one of Maine's most-photographed buildings. Driving down Summer Street (Rte. 35), midway between the downtowns of Kennebunk and Kennebunkport, it's hard to miss the yellow-and-white Federal mansion with gobs of gingerbread and Gothic Revival spires and arches. Built in 1826 by shipbuilder George Bourne as a wedding gift for his wife, the Kennebunk landmark remained in the family until 1983.

Cape Porpoise

When your mind's eye conjures an idyllic lobster-fishing village, it probably looks a lot like Cape Porpoise, only 2.5 miles from busy Dock Square. Follow Route 9 eastward from Kennebunkport; when Route 9 turns north, continue straight and take Pier Road to its end. From the small parking area, you'll see lobster boats at anchor, a slew of working wharves, and 19th-century **Goat Island Light,** now automated, directly offshore.

Local History Museums

Occupying four restored 19th-century buildings in downtown Kennebunk, including the 1825 William Lord store, **The Brick Store Museum** (117 Main St., Kennebunk, 207/985-4802, www.brickstoremuseum.org, 10am-4:30pm Tues.-Fri., 10am-1pm Sat., $5 donation) has garnered a reputation for unusual exhibits: a century of wedding dresses, a two-century history of volunteer firefighting, and life in southern Maine during the Civil War. The museum encourages appreciation for the surrounding Kennebunk Historic District with 50-90-minute **architectural walking tours** ($5), usually May-mid-October but call for a current schedule. If the schedule doesn't suit, the museum sells a walk-it-yourself booklet ($16) and a simple map($5).

Owned and maintained by the Kennebunkport Historical Society, **The Nott House** (8 Maine St., Kennebunkport, 207/967-2751, www.kporthistory.org), a mid-19th-century Greek Revival mansion filled with Victorian furnishings, is open for 45-minute guided tours, which depart on the quarter hour, 11:15am-2:15pm Thursday-Saturday in July-August; $10. Be sure to visit the restored gardens. Hour-long architectural walking tours ($10 adults) of the Kennebunkport Historic District depart from the Nott House (11am Thurs.-Sat., July-Aug., $10). Combination tickets for the house and walking tour are $15. At the house, you can buy a guidebook ($4) for a do-it-yourself tour.

◖ Dock Square

Even if you're not a shopper, make it a point to meander through the heart of Kennebunkport's shopping district, where onetime fishing shacks have been restored and renovated into upscale shops, boutiques, galleries, and dining spots. Some shops, especially those on upper floors, offer fine harbor views. If you're willing to poke around a bit, you'll find some unusual items that make distinctive souvenirs or gifts—pottery, vintage clothing, books, specialty foods, and yes, T-shirts.

◖ St. Anthony's Franciscan Monastery

Long ago, 35,000 Native Americans used this part of town as a summer camp. So did a group of Lithuanian Franciscan monks who in 1947 fled war-ravaged Europe and acquired the 200-acre St. Anthony's Franciscan Monastery (Beach St., Kennebunk, 207/967-2011). They ran a high school here 1956-1969, and the monks still occupy the handsome Tudor great house, but the well-tended grounds (sprinkled with shrines and a recently restored sculpture created by Vytautas Jonynas for the Vatican Pavilion at the 1964 World's Fair) are open to the public sunrise-sunset daily. A short path leads from the monastery area to a peaceful gazebo overlooking the Kennebunk River. Pets and bikes are not allowed; public restrooms are available.

ENTERTAINMENT AND EVENTS
Performing Arts

MaineStage Shakespeare (www.mainestage-shakespeare.com) performs the bard's works free in Kennebunk's Lafayette Park.

Live professional summer theater is on tap at the **Arundel Barn Playhouse** (53 Old Post Rd., Arundel, 207/985-5552, www.arundelbarnplayhouse.com, $30-42), with productions staged in a renovated 1888 barn June-September.

River Tree Arts (RTA)

The area's cultural spearhead is River Tree Arts (35 Western Ave., Kennebunk, 207/967-9120, www.rivertreearts.org), a volunteer-driven organization that sponsors concerts, classes, workshops, exhibits, and educational programs throughout the year.

Festivals and Events

The **Kennebunkport Festival** in early June celebrates art and food with exhibits, social events, food and wine tastings, celebrity chef dinners, and live music. The first two weekends of December mark the festive **Christmas Prelude,** during which spectacular decorations adorn historic homes, candle-toting carolers stroll through the Kennebunks, stores have special sales, and Santa Claus arrives via lobster boat.

Kennebunk Parks and Recreation sponsors **Concerts in the Park,** a weekly series of free concerts 6:30pm-7:30pm Wednesday late June-mid-August in Rotary Park on Water Street. **Third Friday ArtWalks** are held from June through September in downtown Kennebunk.

The Colony Hotel offers a **summer concert series** on Sunday afternoons ($5).

SHOPPING

Lots of small, attractive boutiques surround **Dock Square,** the hub of Kennebunkport, and flow over the bridge into Kennbunk's Lower Village. Gridlock often develops in midsummer. Avoid driving through here at the height of the season. Take your time and walk, bike, or ride the local trolleys. This is just a sampling of the shopping opportunities.

Antiques and Art

English, European, and American furniture and architectural elements and garden accessories are just a sampling of what you'll find at **Antiques on Nine** (Rte. 9, Lower Village, Kennebunk, 207/967-0626). Another good place for browsing high-end antiques as well as home accents is **Hurlburt Designs** (Rte. 9, Lower Village, Kennebunk, 207/967-4110). More than 30 artists are represented at **Wright Gallery** (Pier Rd., Cape Porpoise, 207/967-5053).

Jean Briggs represents nearly 100 artists at her topflight **Mast Cove Galleries** (Maine St. and Mast Cove Lane, Kennebunkport, 207/967-3453, www.mastcove.com), in a handsome Greek Revival house near the Graves Memorial Library. Prices vary widely, so don't be surprised if you spot something affordable. The gallery often sponsors 2.5-hour evening jazz concerts in July-August ($15 donation includes light refreshments). Call for a schedule. **The Gallery on Chase Hill** (10 Chase Hill Rd., Kennebunkport, 207/967-0049), in the stunningly restored Captain Chase House, mounts rotating exhibits and represents a wide variety of Maine and New England artists. It's a sibling of the **Maine Art Gallery** (14 Western Ave., Kennebunkport, 207/967-0049, www.maine-art.com), which is right down the street. **Compliments** (Dock Sq., Kennebunkport, 207/967-2269) has a truly unique and fun collection of contemporary fine American crafts, with an emphasis on glass and ceramic ware.

Cape Porpoise Outfitters (8 Langsford Rd., Cape Porpoise, 207/200-3737) is hip enough to get a nod from *GQ.* Jared Paul Stern has filled a huge red barn with vintage Americana, from books to clothing, nautical doodads to military artifacts. This is no junk shop; it's a curated collection that earns points for cultural cool.

Specialty Shops

Since 1968, **Port Canvas** (9 Ocean Ave., Kennebunkport, 207/985-9765 or 800/333-6788) has been turning out the best in durable cotton-canvas products. Need a new double-bottomed tote bag? It's here. Also available are golf-bag covers, belts, computer cases, day packs, and, of course, duffel bags.

Quilt fans should make time to visit **Mainely Quilts** (108 Summer St./Rte. 35, Kennebunk, 207/985-4250), behind the Waldo Emerson Inn. The shop has a nice selection of contemporary and antique quilts.

Most of the clothing shops clustered around Dock Square are rather pricey. Not so **Arbitrage** (28 Dock Sq., Kennebunkport, 207/967-9989), which combines designer consignment clothing with new fashions, vintage designer costume jewelry, shoes, and handbags.

Irresistible eye-dazzling costume jewelry, hair ornaments, handbags, lotions, cards, and other delightful finds fill every possible space at **Dannah** (123 Ocean Ave., Kennebunkport, 207/967-8640), in the Breakwater Spa building, with free customer-only parking in the rear.

For a good read, stop by **Kennebooks** (149 Port Rd., Lower Village, Kennebunk, 207/967-6136), which carries books and a whole lot more.

Scalawags is a bonanza for pet owners, with wonderful presents to bring home to furry pals. If traveling with your pooch, ask about local pet-friendly parks, inns, and restaurants, as well as favorite places for walkies.

RECREATION
Parks and Preserves

Take precautions against disease-carrying mosquitoes and ticks when exploring preserves. Thanks to a dedicated coterie of year-round and summer residents, the foresighted **Kennebunkport Conservation Trust** (KCT, 57 Gravelly Brook Rd., Kennebunkport, 207/967-3465, www.kporttrust.org), founded in 1974, has become a nationwide model for land-trust organizations. The KCT has managed to preserve from development several hundred acres of land, including 11 small islands off Cape Porpoise Harbor, and most of this acreage is accessible to the public, especially with a sea kayak. The trust has even assumed ownership of 7.7-acre Goat Island, with its distinctive lighthouse visible from Cape Porpoise, and other coastal vantage points. Check the website for special events and activities.

VAUGHN'S ISLAND PRESERVE

To visit Vaughn's Island you'll need to do a little planning, tide-wise, since the 96-acre island is about 600 feet offshore. Consult a tide calendar and aim for low tide close to the new moon or full moon, when the most water drains away. Allow yourself an hour or so before and after low tide, but no longer, or you may need a boat rescue. Wear treaded rubber boots, since the crossing is muddy and slippery

with rockweed. Keep an eye on your watch and explore the ocean (east) side of the island, along the beach. It's worth the effort, and there's a great view of Goat Island Light off to the east. From downtown Kennebunkport, take Main Street to Wildes District Road. Continue to Shore Road (also called Turbat's Creek Road), go 0.6 mile, jog left 0.2 mile more, and park in the tiny lot at the end.

EMMONS PRESERVE

Also under Kennebunkport Conservation Trust's stewardship, the Emmons Preserve has three trails (blazed blue, yellow, and pink) meandering through 146 acres of woods and fields on the edge of Batson's River (also called Gravelly Brook). The yellow trail gives best access to the water. Fall colors here are brilliant, birdlife is abundant, and you can do a loop in half an hour. But why rush? This is a wonderful oasis in the heart of Kennebunkport. From Dock Square, take North Street to Beachwood Avenue (right turn) to Gravelly Brook Road (left turn). The trailhead is on the left.

PICNIC ROCK

About 1.5 miles up the Kennebunk River from the ocean, Picnic Rock is the centerpiece of the **Butler Preserve,** a 14-acre enclave managed by The Nature Conservancy. Well named, the rock is a great place for a picnic and a swim, but don't count on being alone. A short trail loops through the preserve. Consider bringing a canoe or kayak (or renting one) and paddling with the tide past beautiful homes and the Cape Arundel Golf Club. From Lower Village Kennebunk, take Route 35 west and hang a right onto Old Port Road. When the road gets close to the Kennebunk River, watch for a Nature Conservancy oak-leaf sign on the right. Parking is along Old Port Road; walk down through the preserve to Picnic Rock, right on the river.

© TOM NANGLE

The Kennebunks have a number of prime swaths of sand.

Water Sports

BEACHES

Ah, the beaches. The Kennebunks are well endowed with sand but not with parking spaces. Parking permits are required, and you need a separate pass for each town. Many lodgings provide free permits for their guests—be sure to ask when making room reservations. You can avoid the parking nightmare altogether by hopping aboard the Intown Trolley, which goes right by the major beaches.

The main beaches in **Kennebunk** (east to west, stretching about two miles) are 3,346-foot-long Gooch's (the most popular), Kennebunk (locally called Middle Beach or Rocks Beach), and Mother's (a smallish beach next to Lords Point, where there's also a playground). Lifeguards are on duty at Gooch's and Mother's Beaches July-Labor Day. Ask locally about a couple of other beach options. Mid-June-mid-September you'll need to buy a parking permit ($15 per day, $50 per week, $100 for

the season) from the Kennebunk Town Hall (4 Summer St., 207/985-3675) or from HB Provisions (Western Ave., Lower Village).

Kennebunkport's claim to beach fame is three-mile-long Goose Rocks Beach, one of the loveliest in the area. Parking spaces are scarce, and a permit is required. Permits ($12 per day, $50 per week, $100 for the season) are available from the Kennebunkport Police Station (101 Main St., 207/967-4243, 24 hours daily), Kennebunkport Town Hall (6 Elm St.), and Goose Rocks General Store (3 Dyke Rd., 207/967-4541). To reach the beach, take Route 9 from Dock Square east and north to Dyke Road (Clock Farm Corner). Turn right and continue to the end (King's Hwy.).

The prize for tiniest beach goes to Colony (officially Arundel) Beach, near The Colony resort complex. It's close to many Kennebunkport lodgings and an easy walk from Dock Square; no permit is necessary.

SOUTHERN COAST

BOAT EXCURSIONS

Join Captain Gary aboard the 87-foot *Nick's Chance* (4 Western Ave., Lower Village, Kennebunk, 207/967-5507 or 800/767-2628, www.firstchancewhalewatch.com, $48 adults, $28 ages 3-12, $10 under age 3, cash only) for 4.5-hour whale-watching trip to Jeffrey's Ledge, weather permitting. The destination is the summer feeding grounds for finbacks, humpbacks, minkes, the rare blue whale, and the endangered right whale. The boat departs once or twice daily late June-early September, weekends only spring and fall, from Performance Marine, behind Bartley's Restaurant, in Kennebunk Lower Village.

Under the same ownership and departing from the same location is the 65-foot open lobster boat *Kylie's Chance,* which departs four times daily in July-August for 1.5-hour scenic lobster cruises ($20 adults, $15 ages 3-12, cash only); the schedule is reduced in spring and fall. A lobstering demonstration is given on most trips but never on the evening one.

The handsome 55-foot gaff-rigged schooner *Eleanor* (Arundel Wharf, 43 Ocean Ave., Kennebunkport, 207/967-8809, www.gwi.net/schoonersails), built by its captain, Rich Woodman, heads out for two-hour sails ($45 pp), weather and tides willing, 1-3 times daily during the summer. Also operating out of the same office and dock is the *Porpuse,* a fancy lobster boat, which transports up to six people per trip to Goat Island Light, allowing them time to tour the property and climb the tower. Call for the schedule, as the boat goes only at high tide. The cost is $60 per person, cash or check.

CANOEING, KAYAKING, AND PADDLEBOARDING

Explore the Kennebunk River by canoe or kayak. **Kennebunkport Marina** (67 Ocean Ave., Kennebunkport, 207/967-3411, www.kennebunkportmarina.com) rents canoes and single kayaks ($30 for two hours, $50 per half day) and double kayaks ($50 for two hours, $70 per half day). Check the tide before you depart, and plan your trip to paddle with it rather than against it.

Coastal Maine Kayak (8 Western Ave., Lower Village, Kennebunk, 207/967-6065, www.coastalmainekayak.com) offers a day-long guided Cape Porpoise Lighthouse Tour ($85), including guide, instruction, equipment, and lunch; other options are available. Rental kayaks are $35 for three hours, $60 full day, and $350 per week; doubles are $60, $80, and $500.

Take a half-day sea kayaking tour ($50 pp) or do it yourself with a rental kayak or paddleboard (from $35) with **Southern Maine Kayaks** (888/925-7495, www.southernmainekayaks.com).

© HILARY NANGLE

Head out on a whale-watching trip from Dock Square.

© TOM NANGLE

The Colony Hotel is one of the last historical grand resorts still operating on the Maine coast.

SURFING AND PADDLEBOARDING

If you want to catch a wave, stop by **Aquaholics Surf Shop** (166 Port Rd., Kennebunk, 207/967-8650, www.aquaholicsurf.com). The shop has boards, wetsuits, and related gear both for sale and rental, and it offers lessons and surf camps.

Bicycling

Coastal Maine Kayak (8 Western Ave., Lower Village, Kennebunk, 207/967-6065, www.coastalmainekayak.com) rents bikes starting at $10 per hour or $35 per day.

Golf

Three 18-hole golf courses make the sport a big deal in the area. **Cape Arundel Golf Club** (19 River Rd., Kennebunkport, 207/967-3494), established in 1897, and **Webhannet Golf Club** (8 Central Ave., Kennebunk, 207/967-2061), established in 1902, are semiprivate and open to nonmembers; call for tee times at least 24 hours ahead. In nearby Arundel, **Dutch Elm Golf Course** (5 Brimstone Rd., Arundel, 207/282-9850) is a public course with rentals, pro shop, and putting greens.

ACCOMMODATIONS

Rates listed are for peak season; most stay open through Christmas Prelude.

Inns and Hotels

Graciously dominating its 11-acre spread at the mouth of the Kennebunk River, **The Colony Hotel** (140 Ocean Ave. at King's Hwy., Kennebunkport, 207/967-3331 or 800/552-2363, www.thecolonyhotel.com/maine, $180) springs right out of a bygone era, and its distinctive cupola is an area landmark. It has had a longtime commitment to the environment, with recycling, waste-reduction, and educational programs. There's a special feeling here, with cozy corners for reading, lawns and gardens for strolling, an ocean-view heated swimming pool, room service, putting green, tennis privileges at the exclusive River Club, bike rentals, massage therapy, and lawn games. The price of rooms includes breakfast. Pets are $30 per night. There are no in-room TVs in the main inn.

The White Barn Inn and its siblings specialize in the ultrahigh-end boutique inn market, with four in this category. Most renowned is the ultraexclusive **White Barn Inn** (37 Beach Ave., Kennebunk, 207/967-2321, www.whitebarninn.com, from $465). Also part of the empire are **The Beach House Inn** (211 Beach Ave., Kennebunk, 207/967-3850, www.beachhseinn. com, from $209), **The Breakwater Inn, Hotel, and Spa** (127 Ocean Ave., Kennebunkport, 207/967-3118, www.thebreakwaterinn.com, from $289), **The Yachtsman Lodge and Marina** (Ocean Ave., Kennebunkport, 207/967-2511, www.yachtsmanlodge.com, from $309), and two restaurants. Guest rooms in all properties have air-conditioning, phones, satellite TV, and video and CD players; bikes and canoes are available for guests. Rates include bountiful continental breakfasts and afternoon tea, but check out the off-season packages, especially if you want to dine at one of the restaurants. All but the Beach House are within walking distance of Dock Square.

The White Barn Inn is the most exclusive, with Relais & Châteaux status. It's home to one of the best restaurants in the *country.* Many rooms have fireplaces and marble baths with separate steam showers and whirlpool tubs (you can even arrange for a butler-drawn bath). Service is impeccable, and nothing has been overlooked in terms of amenities. There's an outdoor heated European-style infinity pool, where lunch is available, weather permitting, as well as a full-service spa. The inn also has a Hinckley Talaria-44 yacht available for charter.

The Beach House Inn faces Middle Beach and is less formal than the White Barn (splurge on upper-floor guest rooms with views). The Breakwater, at the mouth of the Kennebunk River, comprises a beautifully renovated historical inn with wraparound porches and an adjacent, more modern, newly renovated building with guest rooms and a full-service spa. The complex is also home to Stripers Restaurant. Finally, there's the Yachtsman, an innovative blend of a motel and bed-and-breakfast, with all rooms opening onto patios facing the river and the marina where George H. W. Bush keeps his boat. Pets are allowed here by advance reservation for $25 per night.

All but two guest rooms at the **Cape Arundel Inn** (208 Ocean Ave., Kennebunkport, 207/967-2125, www.capearundelinn.com, Mar.-Jan. 1, $335-460) overlook crashing surf and the Bush estate. The compound comprises the shingle-style main inn building, the Rockbound motel-style building, and the Carriage House Loft, a large suite on the upper floor of the carriage house; breakfast is included. All guest rooms are air-conditioned and most have fireplaces. Bikes and beach passes, towels, and chairs are provided. Every table in the inn's restaurant (entrées $27-40) has an ocean view.

Families, especially, favor the sprawling riverfront **Nonantum Resort** (95 Ocean Ave., Kennebunkport, 207/967-4050 or 888/205-1555, www.nonantumresort.com, from $249) complex, which dates from 1884. It includes a bit of everything, from gently updated rooms and suites in the main building to modern family suites with kitchenettes in the newer Portside building, where some third-floor rooms have ocean views. Recreational amenities include a small outdoor heated pool, docking facilities, lobster-boat and sailing tours, fishing charters, and kayak rentals. A slew of activities are offered daily, including a children's program. All 115 guest rooms have air-conditioning, Wi-Fi, and TVs; some have refrigerators. Rates include a full breakfast. The water-view dining room is also open for dinner and, in July-August, lunch. Packages, many of which include dinner,

© HILARY NANGLE

Guests staying at the Cape Arundel Inn have views over the open Atlantic and the Bush estate at Walker Point.

are a good choice. Note that weddings take place here almost every weekend.

The **Kennebunkport Resort Collection** (www.kennebunkportresortcollection.com) is made up of about half a dozen distinctive, luxury accommodations in the area, all with the expected amenities. A seasonal dinner shuttle provides transportation between them. Fanciest is **Hidden Pond** (354 Goose Rocks Rd., Kennebunkport, 888/967-9050, from $670), which shares amenities with nearby **Tides Beach Club** (254 Kings Hwy., Kennebunkport, 855/632-3324, www.tidesbeachclubmaine.com, from $265). The family-oriented Hidden Pond resort, tucked in the woods about a mile from Goose Rocks Beach, comprises chic designer-Victorianesque cottages and bungalows, gardens, a spa, a wellness center, outdoor pools, a pool grill, and the fine-dining restaurant Earth. The renovated Victorian Tides Beach Club is a hip boutique hotel with restaurant/lounge on

Goose Rocks Beach. A tender oversees beach chairs and umbrellas, provides water, and even delivers lunch.

Location, location, location: The meticulously renovated 1899 **C Kennebunkport Inn** (1 Dock Sq., Kennebunkport, 207/967 2621, from $169) comprises three buildings in the heart of Dock Square. It also has an excellent restaurant, One Dock, as well as piano bar. Rates include a continental breakfast.

Bed-and-Breakfasts

Three of Kennebunkport's loveliest inns are rumored to have been owned by brothers-in-law, all of whom were sea captains. Rivaling the White Barn Inn for service, decor, amenities, and overall luxury is the three-story **C Captain Lord Mansion** (Pleasant St., Kennebunkport, 207/967-3141 or 800/522-3141, www.captainlord.com, from $299), which is one of the finest bed-and-breakfasts

© HILARY NANGLE

The Nonantum Resort is an excellent family resort with a wide array of programs and facilities.

anywhere. And no wonder: Innkeepers Rick and Bev Litchfield have been at it since 1978, and they're never content to rest on their laurels. Each year the inn improves upon seeming perfection. If you want to be pampered and stay in a meticulously decorated and historical bed-and-breakfast with marble bathrooms (heated floors, many with double whirlpool tubs), fireplaces, original artwork, phones, TVs, Wi-Fi, air-conditioning in all guest rooms, and even a few cedar closets, look no further. A multicourse breakfast is served to shared tables. Bicycles as well as beach towels and chairs are available. Afternoon treats are provided.

The elegant Federal-style **Captain Jefferds Inn** (5 Pearl St., Kennebunkport, 207/967-2311 or 800/839-6844, www.captainjefferdsinn. com, $199-389), in the historic district, provides the ambience of a real captain's house. Each of the 15 guest rooms and suites (11 in the main house and 4 more in the carriage house) has plush linens, fresh flowers, down comforters, TVs and DVD players, CD players, Wi-Fi, and air-conditioning; some have fireplaces, whirlpool tubs, and other luxuries. A three-course breakfast and afternoon tea are included. Five rooms are dog-friendly, at $30 per day per dog; pet sitting is available.

The **Captain Fairfield Inn** (8 Pleasant St., Kennebunkport, www.captainfairfield.com, from $280) is perhaps the most modest architecturally of the three, but it doesn't scrimp on amenities. Guest rooms are divided between traditional and contemporary decor, but all have flat-screen TVs, air-conditioning, and Wi-Fi; some have gas fireplaces, double whirlpools, and rainfall showers. The lovely grounds are a fine place to retreat for a snooze in the hammock or a game of croquet. Rates include a four-course breakfast and afternoon cookies.

The original 1860s Greek Revival architecture of the **English Meadows Inn** (141 Port Rd.,

Lower Village, Kennebunk, 207/967-5766, www.englishmeadowsinn.com, from $249) was married to the Victorian Queen Anne style later in the century, but the interior decor is contemporary and clutter free, with accents such as Asian art, Picasso lithographs, and art deco lighting. Guest rooms are split between the main house, the carriage house, and a pet-friendly ($30) two-bedroom cottage. All have flat-screen TVs, some have fireplaces or whirlpool tubs. Rates include a full breakfast and afternoon snacks.

Slip away from the crowds at the Gott family's antiques-filled **C Bufflehead Cove Inn** (B18 Bufflehead Cove Lane, Kennebunkport, 207/967-3879, www.buffleheadcove.com, from $165), a secluded riverfront home in the woods, less than one mile from K'port's action. Really, with a location like this and pampering service, you just might not want to stray from the front porch or dock. Rooms have Wi-Fi, flat-screen TVs, and air-conditioning; some have fireplaces and whirlpool tubs. Rates include a full breakfast and afternoon treats and use of beach chairs, umbrellas, and passes.

Neighboring the Wedding Cake House, **The Waldo Emerson Inn** (108 Summer St./ Rte. 35, Kennebunk, 207/985-4250, www. waldoemersoninn.com, from $170) has a charming colonial feel, as it should, since the main section was built in 1784. Poet Ralph Waldo Emerson spent many a summer here; it was his great-uncle's home. Three of the six attractive guest rooms have working fireplaces. Rates include a full breakfast. Quilters, take note: In the barn is Mainely Quilts, a well-stocked quilt shop.

Traveling with a pooch? **The Hounds Tooth Inn** (82 Summer St., Kennebunk, 207/985-0117, www.houndstoothinn.biz, from $165, from $30 per pet) extends a welcome paw, allowing dogs in public rooms (but not the kitchen) and providing a fenced-in play area. Rates include a full breakfast.

Motels

Patricia Mason is the ninth-generation innkeeper at **The Seaside Motor Inn** (80 Beach Ave., Kennebunk, 207/967-4461 or 800/967-4461, www.kennebunkbeach.com, $239-299), a property that has been in her family since 1667. What a location! The 22-room motel is the only truly beachfront property in the area. Rooms are spacious, with TVs, Wi-Fi, air-conditioning, and refrigerators. Guests have use of an ocean-view hot tub and bicycles. A continental breakfast is included in the rates. Kids age 12 and younger stay free.

Second-generation innkeepers David and Paula Reid keep the **Fontenay Terrace Motel** (128 Ocean Ave., Kennebunkport, 207/967-3556, www.fontenaymotel.com, from $140) spotless. It borders a tidal inlet and has a private grassy and shaded lawn, perfect for retreating from the hubbub of busy Kennebunkport. Each of the eight guest rooms has air-conditioning, a mini-fridge, a microwave, Wi-Fi, cable TV, and a phone; some have water views. A small beach is 300 yards away, and it's a pleasant one-mile walk to Dock Square.

The clean and simple **Cape Porpoise Motel** (12 Mills Rd./Rte. 9, Cape Porpoise, 207/967-3370, www.capeporpoisemotel.com, from $139) is a short walk from the harbor. All rooms have TV and air-conditioning, and some have kitchenettes; rates include a continental breakfast, with homemade baked goods, fresh fruit, cereals, and bagels. Also available by the week or month are efficiencies with full kitchens, phones, and one or more bedrooms.

Here's a bargain: The nonprofit **Franciscan Guest House** (28 Beach Ave., Kennebunk, 207/967-4865, www.franciscanguesthouse. com), on the grounds of the monastery, has accommodations spread among two buildings and three other Tudor-style cottages. Decor is vintage 1970s, frills are few, and yes, it's in need of updating, but there are some nice amenities, including TVs, air-conditioning, a saltwater pool, Wi-Fi, and beach passes. The location is within walking distance of the beach and Dock Square. A continental breakfast is included in the rates (hot buffet available, $3), and a buffet dinner is often available (around $17). There is no daily maid service, but fresh towels are provided. Rooms are $89-175, and 1-3-bedroom suites are $99-240; no credit cards.

FOOD

Hours are for peak season, when reservations are advised. It's always wise to confirm. The Kennebunkport Resort Collection operates a dining shuttle between its properties in Kennebunkport and Goose Rocks Beach. It's free for guests at its hotels, but anyone can hop aboard for $5.

Get the lowdown on K'port's food scene on a walking or trolley culinary tasting tour with **Maine Foodie Tours** (207/233-7485, www. mainefoodietours.com). Tickets, available online, cost about $50 for either.

Local Flavors

All Day Breakfast (55 Western Ave./Rte. 9, Lower Village, Kennebunk, 207/967-5132, 7am-1:30pm Mon.-Fri., 7am-2pm Sat.-Sun. mid-Jan.-mid-Dec.) is a favorite meeting spot, offering such specialties as invent-your-own omelets and crepes, Texas French toast, and the ADB sandwich.

H. B. Provisions (15 Western Ave., Lower Village, Kennebunk, 207/967-5762, www.hb-provisions.com, 6am-10pm daily) has an excellent wine selection, along with plenty of picnic supplies, newspapers, and all the typical general-store inventory. It also serves breakfast and prepares hot and cold sandwiches, salads, and wraps.

Equal parts fancy food and wine store and gourmet café, **Cape Porpoise Kitchen** (Rte. 9, Cape Porpoise, 207/967-1150, 7am-6pm daily) sells sandwiches, salads, prepared foods, desserts, and everything to go with.

Pair a fine wine with light fare at **Old Vines** (141 Port Rd., Lower Village, Kennebunk, 207/967-5766, 5pm-11pm Wed.-Mon.), an Old World-meets-New World European-style wine bar and tapas restaurant housed in a renovated barn. The food is creative and excellent.

Prefer ales? **Federal Jack's** (8 Western Ave., Lower Village, Kennebunk, 207/967-4322, www.federaljacks.com, 11am-12:30am) is the brewpub that gave birth to the Shipyard label. Aim for a seat on the riverfront deck. Call in advance for a tour, and if you're serious about brewing, ask about the Maine Brewing Vacation.

The **Kennebunk Farmers Market** sets up shop 8am-1pm Saturday mid-May-mid-October in the Grove Street municipal parking lot off Route 1 (adjacent to Village Pharmacy).

Family Favorites

A bit off the beaten track is **Lucas on 9** (62 Mills Rd./Rte. 9, Cape Porpoise, 207/967-0039, www.lucason9.com, noon-9pm Wed.-Mon., $9-22), a family-friendly restaurant operated by the Lane family. Chef Jonathan Lane makes everything from scratch and delivers on his mother Deborah's mission of "Good American food at affordable prices." Jonathan's travels have infused his preparations with more than a bow toward his work on Southern riverboats (Louisiana spicy crab soup, bread pudding with whiskey).

Burgers, pizza, sandwiches, even a turkey dinner with the trimmings—almost everything on the menu is less than $12 at **Duffy's Tavern & Grill** (4 Main St., Kennebunk, 207/985-0050, www.duffyskennebunk.com, from 11am daily). Extremely popular with locals, Duffy's is inside a renovated mill in Lafayette Center. It's an inviting space with exposed beams, gleaming woodwork, brick walls, and big windows framing the Mousam River. And if you want to catch the game while you eat, big-screen high-def TVs make it easy.

Casual Dining

The views complement the food at **Hurricane Restaurant** (29 Dock Sq., Kennebunkport, 207/967-9111, www.hurricanerestaurant.com, from 11:30 daily, entrées $20-50). Thanks to a Dock Square location and a dining room that literally hangs over the river, it reels in the crowds for both lunch and dinner.

Eat well and feel good about it at **Bandaloop** (2 Dock Sq., Kennebunkport, 207/967-4994, www.bandaloop.biz, 5pm-10pm Sun.-Thurs., 5pm-11pm Fri.-Sat. year-round, $17-29), a hip, vibrant restaurant where chef-owner W. Scott Lee likes to push boundaries. Lee named the restaurant for author Tom Robbins's fictional tribe that knew the secret to eternal life. Lee believes the secret is fresh, local, organic, and cruelty free. Selections vary from meats and fish to vegetarian and vegan prepared with creativity.

Floor-to-ceiling windows frame the Kennebunk River breakwater, providing perfect views for those indulging at **Stripers** (Breakwater Inn, 127 Ocean Ave., Kennebunkport, 207/967-5333, from noon daily), another White Barn Inn sibling, where fish and seafood are the specialties. Most entrées range $23-31. Dress is casual; valet parking is available.

Dine in the heart of the action at **Dock Square** (1 Dock Sq., Kennebunkport, 207/967-2621, www.onedock.com, from 5:30pm daily), in the Kennebunkport Inn. Choose from patio dining (in season), the cozy dining room, or pub, with live entertainment nightly in season. Although there are small plates, most entrées run $23-31.

Chef Peter and his wife, Kate, operate **Pier 77** (77 Pier Rd., Cape Porpoise, 207/967-8500, www.pier77restaurant.com, 11:30am-2:30pm and 5pm-9pm daily, entrées $18-32), which overlooks Cape Porpoise Harbor with lobster boats hustling to and fro. The menu varies from paella to seafood mixed grill. There's frequent live entertainment, which can make conversation difficult. Reservations are advisable. Practically hidden downstairs is the always packed **Ramp Bar and Grille** (11:30am-9pm daily), with lighter fare as well as the full menu and a sports-pub decor.

Local is the key word at **50 Local** (50 Main St., Kennebunk, 207/985-0850, www.localkennebunk.com, from 5pm daily, $10-36), a bright spot in downtown Kennebunk specializing in local and organic fare. The menu changes daily, but it's easy to cobble together a meal here that fits your appetite and budget.

Fine Dining

European country cuisine reigns at **On the Marsh** (46 Western Ave./Rte. 9, Lower Village, Kennebunk, 207/967-2299, www.onthemarsh.com, from 5:30pm daily, entrées $25-40), a restored barn overlooking marshlands leading to Kennebunk Beach. Lighter fare is served in the bar. The space is infused with arts and antiques and European touches courtesy of owner Denise Rubin, an interior designer with a passion for the continent. Dining locations include the two-level dining area, an "owner's table" with a chef's menu, and in the kitchen. Quiet piano music adds to the elegant but unstuffy ambience on weekends; service is attentive. Reservations are essential in midsummer.

Destination Dining

One of Maine's biggest splurges and worth every penny is **⬛ The White Barn Inn** (37 Beach Ave., Kennebunkport, 207/967-2321, www.whitebarninn.com, 6:30pm-9:30pm daily), with haute cuisine and haute prices in a haute-rustic barn. In summer, don't be surprised to run into members of the senior George Bush clan (probably at the back window table). Soft piano music accompanies impeccable service and chef Jonathan Cartwright's outstanding four-course (plus extras) fixed-price menu (about $106 pp, add $58 or $85 for wine pairings). Reservations are essential—well ahead

© HILARY NANGLE

The best fried clams in the Kennebunks come from The Clam Shack, just across the bridge from Dock Square.

during July-August—and you'll need a credit card (cancel 24 hours ahead or you'll be charged). Jackets are required, and no jeans or sneakers are allowed. Although the price is high, the value for the dollar far exceeds that. If you can afford it, dine here.

Also splurge-worthy is **Earth** (at Hidden Pond resort, 354 Goose Rocks Rd., Kennebunkport, 207/967-6550, www.earthathiddenpond.com, from 5:30pm daily, $18-40), where James Beard award-winning Boston restaurateur Ken Orringer hangs his toque in Maine. The farm-to-fork cuisine includes handmade pastas, house-made charcuteries, wood-oven pizzas, and entrées such as local seafood paella and grilled skirt steak. The dining room is rustic, and the garden views are sublime.

Lobster and Clams

Nunan's Lobster Hut (9 Mills Rd., Cape Porpoise, 207/967-4362, www.nunanslobsterhut.com, 5pm-close daily) is an institution. Sure, other places might have better views, but this casual dockside eatery with indoor and outdoor seating has been serving lobsters since 1953.

Adjacent to the bridge connecting Kennebunkport's Dock Square to Kennebunk's Lower Village is another time-tested classic, **The Clam Shack** (Rte. 9, Kennebunkport, 207/967-2560, www.theclamshack.net, lunch and dinner from 11am daily May-Oct.). The tiny take-out stand serves perhaps the state's best lobster rolls, jam-packed with meat and available with either butter or mayo, and deelish fried clams.

Lobster and crab rolls are the specialties at **Port Lobster** (122 Ocean Ave., Kennebunkport, 207/967-2081, www.portlobster.com, 9am-6pm daily), a fresh-fish store just northeast of Dock Square.

Pair your lobster with a view of Goat Island Light at **Cape Pier Chowder House** (79 Pier Rd., Cape Porpoise, 207/967-0123, from 11am daily).

INFORMATION AND SERVICES

The **Kennebunk and Kennebunkport Chamber of Commerce** (17 Western Ave./Rte. 9, Lower Village, Kennebunk, 207/967-0857, www.visitthekennebunks.com) produces an excellent area guide to accommodations, restaurants, area maps, bike maps, tide calendars, recreation, and beach parking permits.

Check out **Louis T. Graves Memorial Public Library** (18 Maine St., Kennebunkport, 207/967-2778, www.graves.lib.me.us) or **Kennebunk Free Library** (112 Main St., 207/985-2173, www.kennebunklibrary.org).

Public restrooms are at Gooch's and Mother's Beaches and at St. Anthony's Franciscan Monastery, the chamber of commerce building (17 Western Ave.), and at the chamber's Dock Square Hospitality Center.

GETTING THERE AND AROUND

Kennebunk is about five miles or 10 minutes via Route 1 from Wells. Kennebunkport is about 6.5 miles or 12 minutes via Routes 1 and 9 from Wells. Kennebunk and Kennebunkport are connected by four miles of Route 9. From Kennebunk to Biddeford, it's about nine miles or 17 minutes via Route 1. Allow longer for summer congestion in each town.

Amtrak's *Downeaster* (800/872-7245, www.thedowneaster.com) connects Boston's North Station with Portland, Maine, with stops in Wells, Saco, and Old Orchard Beach (seasonal). It connects with the seasonal **Shoreline Explorer** (207/324-5762, www.shorelineexplorer.com) trolley system, which operates between York and Kennebunkport. Each town's system is operated separately and has its own fees. The **Shoreline Trolley Line 7/Kennebunk Shuttle** ($1 one way, $3 day pass, $10 12-ride multipass, free for kids under 18) connects Line 4 (serving the Wells Transportation Facility and the *Downeaster*) with downtown Kennebunk, Lower Village, and Kennebunk's beaches.

Shoreline Trolley Line 6/Intown Trolley (207/967-3686, www.intowntrolley.com, $16, $6 ages 3-17) operates as a narrated sightseeing tour throughout Kennebunk and Kennebunkport. It originates in Dock Square and makes regular stops at beaches and other attractions. The entire route takes about 45 minutes, with the driver providing a hefty dose of local history and gossip. Seats are park bench-style. You can get on or off at any stop.

Old Orchard Beach Area

Seven continuous miles of white sand beach have been drawing vacation-oriented folks for generations to the area stretching from Camp Ellis in Saco to Pine Point in Scarborough. Cottage colonies and condo complexes dominate at the extremities, but the center of activity has always been and remains Old Orchard Beach.

In its heyday, **Old Orchard Beach's pier** reached far out into the sea, huge resort hotels lined the sands, and wealthy Victorian folk (including Rose Fitzgerald and Joe Kennedy, who met on these sands in the days when men strolled around in dress suits and women toted parasols) came each summer to see and be seen.

Storms and fires have taken their toll through the years, and the grand resorts have been replaced by endless motels, many of which display "Nous parlons français" signs to welcome the masses of French Canadians who

© HILARY NANGLE

The Pier at Old Orchard Beach has survived since 1898.

arrive each summer. They're joined by young families who come for the sand and surf along with T-shirted and body-pierced young pleasure seekers who come for the nightlife.

Although some residents are pushing for gentrification and a few projects are moving things in that direction, Old Orchard Beach (pop. 8,624) remains somewhat honky-tonk, and most of its visitors would have it no other way. French fries, cotton candy, and beach-accessories shops line the downtown, and as you get closer to the pier, you pass arcades and amusement parks. There's not a kid on earth who wouldn't have fun in Old Orchard—even if some parents might find it all a bit much.

Much more sedate are the villages on the fringes. The **Ocean Park** section of Old Orchard, at the southwestern end of town, was established in 1881 as a religious summer-cottage community. It still offers interdenominational services and vacation Bible school, but it also has an active cultural association that

sponsors concerts, Chautauqua-type lectures, films, and other events throughout the summer. All are open to the public.

South of that is **Camp Ellis.** Begun as a small fishing village named after early settler Thomas Ellis, it is crowded with longtime summer homes that are in a constant battle with the sea. A nearly mile-long granite jetty—designed to keep silt from clogging the Saco River—has taken the blame for massive beach erosion since it was constructed. But the jetty is a favorite spot for wetting a line and for panoramic views off toward Wood Island Light (built in 1808) and Biddeford Pool. Camp Ellis Beach is open to the public, with lifeguards on duty in mid-summer. Parking—scarce on hot days—is $10 per day.

As you head north from Old Orchard, you'll pass **Pine Point,** another longtime community of vacation homes. Services are few, and parking is $10 per day.

Most folks get to Old Orchard by passing

© HILARY NANGLE

You never know who you'll see at Old Orchard Beach.

through **Saco** (pop. 18,482)and **Biddeford** (pop. 21,277), which have long been upstairs-downstairs sister cities, with wealthy mill owners living in Saco and their workers and workplaces in Biddeford. But even those personalities have always been split—congested commercial Route 1 is part of Saco, and the exclusive enclave of Biddeford Pool is, of course, in below-stairs Biddeford.

Saco still has an attractive downtown, with boutiques and stunning homes on Main Street and beyond. Blue-collar Biddeford is working hard to change its mill-town image. It's home to the magnificent Biddeford City Theater and the University of New England, and as a Main Street community it's getting a much-needed sprucing up. Another Biddeford hallmark is its Franco-American tradition, thanks to the French-speaking workers who sustained the textile and shoemaking industries in the 19th century. The mills on the Saco River island

between the two cities are being rehabbed to house restaurants, shops, offices, and condos.

SIGHTS
Saco Museum
Founded in 1866, the Saco Museum (371 Main St., Saco, 207/283-3861, www.dyerlibrarysacomuseum.org, noon-4pm Tues.-Thurs. and Sun., noon-8pm Fri., 10am-4pm Sat. June-Dec., $5 adults, $3 seniors, $2 students and children age seven and older) rotates selections from its outstanding collection, including 18th- and 19th-century paintings, furniture, and other household treasures. Lectures, workshops, and concerts are also part of the annual schedule. Admission is free after 4pm Friday.

◖ Wood Island Lighthouse
The all-volunteer Friends of Wood Island Light (207/200-4552, www.woodislandlighthouse.org) is restoring Maine's second-oldest lighthouse, which was commissioned by President Thomas Jefferson, built in 1808 (reconstructed in 1858) on 35-acre Wood Island, and abandoned in 1986. In July-August the Friends offer 1.5-hour guided tours ($12 pp recommended donation) of the two-story keeper's house and 42-foot-tall stone tower, relating tales of former keepers and their families to bring the site to life. You can even climb the 60 stairs to the tower's lantern room for splendid views. The tour departs from Vine's Landing in Biddeford Pool. Once on the island, it's about a half-mile walk to the site. Reservations are accepted within one week of the tour date; see the website or call for a current schedule.

ENTERTAINMENT
At 6pm every Thursday late June-Labor Day **free concerts** are staged in Old Orchard's Memorial Park, followed by **fireworks** set off by the pier at 9:45pm.

Family concerts and other performances are staged at the outdoor **Seaside Pavilion** (8 Sixth

St., Old Orchard Beach, 207/934-2024, www.seasidepavilion.org).

Ocean Park's **Temple,** a 19th-century octagon that seats more than 800, is the venue for Saturday- or Sunday-night concerts (7:30pm, $12 adults) and many other programs throughout the summer.

Designed by noted architect John Calvin Stevens in 1896, the 500-seat **City Theater** (205 Main St., Biddeford, 207/282-0849, www.citytheater.org) in Biddeford, on the National Register of Historic Places, has been superbly restored, and the acoustics are excellent even when Eva Gray, the resident ghost, mixes it up backstage.

A rainy-day godsend, Saco's **IMAX Theater** (779 Portland Rd./Rte. 1, Saco, 207/282-6234, www.cinemagicmovies.com) has digital sound, stadium seating, a restaurant, and on-line ticketing.

Pair burritos and other Tex-Mex faves with live music at **Bebe's Burritos** (140 Main St., Biddeford, 207/283-4222, www.bebesburritos.com, 6pm-10pm Thurs.-Sun.), with trivia on Sunday nights.

EVENTS

La Kermesse (www.lakermessefestival.com), meaning "the fair" or "the festival," is Biddeford's summer highlight, when nearly 50,000 visitors pour into town Thursday-Sunday on the last full weekend in June to celebrate the town's Franco-American heritage. Local volunteers go all-out to plan block parties, a parade, games, a carnival, live entertainment, and traditional dancing. Then there's *la cuisine franco-américaine;* you can fill up on *boudin, creton, poutine, tourtière, tarte au saumon,* and crepes (although your arteries may rebel).

The **Biddeford Art Walk** (www.biddefordartwalk.com) takes place the last Friday of each month.

In July the parishioners of St. Demetrios Greek Orthodox Church (186 Bradley St., Saco, 207/284-5651) mount the annual **Greek Heritage Festival,** a three-day extravaganza of homemade Greek food, traditional Greek music and dancing, and a crafts fair. Be sure to tour the impressive $1.5 million domed church building.

The beaches come to life in July with the annual **Parade and Sandcastle Contest** in Ocean Park.

One weekend in mid-August, Old Orchard Beach's **Beach Olympics** is a family festival of games, exhibitions, and music benefiting Maine's Special Olympics program.

RECREATION
Parks and Preserves

Take precautions against disease-carrying mosquitoes and ticks when exploring preserves. Saco Bay Trails (www.sacobaytrails.org), a local land trust, has produced a very helpful trail guide ($10) that includes the Saco Heath, the East Point Sanctuary, and more than a dozen other local trails. The Cascade Falls trail, for example, is a half-mile stroll ending at a waterfall. Copies are available at a number of Biddeford and Saco locations, including the Dyer Library, or from Saco Bay Trails. Trail information is also on the organization's website.

EAST POINT SANCTUARY

Owned by Maine Audubon (207/781-2330, www.maineaudubon.org), the 30-acre East Point Sanctuary is a splendid preserve at the eastern end of Biddeford Pool. Crashing surf, beach roses, bayberry bushes, and offshore Wood Island Light are all features of the two-part perimeter trail, which skirts the exclusive Abenakee Club's golf course. Allow at least an hour; even in fog, the setting is dramatic. During spring and fall migrations it's one of southern Maine's prime birding locales, so you'll have plenty of company at those times, and the usual street-side parking may be scarce. It's poorly signposted (perhaps deliberately), so you'll want to follow the directions: From Route 9 (Main Street) in downtown Biddeford, take Route 9/208 (Pool Road) southeast about five miles to the Route 208 turnoff to Biddeford Pool. Go 0.6 mile on Route 208 (Bridge Road) and then turn left onto Mile Stretch Road. Continue to Lester B. Orcutt Boulevard, turn left, and go to the end. Be careful: There's poison ivy on the point.

THE HEATH

Owned by The Nature Conservancy, 1,000-plus-acre Saco Heath Preserve is the nation's southernmost "raised coalesced bog," where peat accumulated through eons into two above-water dome shapes that eventually merged into a single natural feature. A bit of esoterica: It's the home of the rare Hessel's hair-streak butterfly. Pick up a map at the parking area and follow the mile-long self-guided trail through the woods and then into the heath via a boardwalk. The best time to visit is early-mid-October, when the heath and woodland colors are positively brilliant and insects are on the wane. You're likely to see deer and perhaps even spot a moose. The preserve entrance is on Route 112 (Buxton Road), two miles west of I-95. Pets are not allowed in the preserve.

FERRY BEACH STATE PARK

When the weather's hot, arrive early at Ferry Beach State Park (95 Bay View Rd., off Rte. 9, Saco, 207/283-0067, $6 nonresident adult, $4 Maine resident adult, $2 nonresident seniors, $1 ages 5-11), a pristine beach backed by dune grass on Saco Bay. In the 117-acre park are changing rooms, restrooms, a lifeguard, picnic tables, and five easy interconnected nature trails winding through woodlands, marshlands, and dunes. Later in the day, keep the insect repellent handy. It's open daily late May-late September but accessible all year; trail markers are removed in winter.

Golf

Tee off at the **Biddeford-Saco Country Club** (101 Old Orchard Rd., Saco, 207/282-5883) or the challenging 18-hole par-71 **Dunegrass Golf Club** (200 Wild Dunes Way, Old Orchard Beach, 207/934-4513 or 800/521-1029).

Water Sports

Moose County Music & Surf (67 E. Grand Ave., Old Orchard Beach, 207/729-1656, www.moosecounty.us) rents surfboards ($10 for one hour, $25 for three hours), wetsuits for $5, and kayaks ($20 for one hour, $35 for two hours).

Gone with the Wind (Yates St., Biddeford Pool, 207/283-8446, www.gwtwonline.com) offers two tours, afternoon and sunset, with prices varying with the number of people on the tour (for two people it's about $85 pp). Wetsuits are supplied. The most popular trip is to Beach Island. Also available are rentals ($40 half day, $65 full day).

ACCOMMODATIONS

The area has hundreds of beds—mostly in motel-style lodgings. The chamber of commerce is the best resource for motels, cottages, and the area's more than 3,000 campsites. The rates noted are for peak season.

The Old Orchard Beach Inn (6 Portland Ave., Old Orchard Beach, 207/934-5834 or 877/700-6624, www.oldorchardbeachinn.com, year-round, $135-200) was rescued from ruin, restored, and reopened in 2000. Built in 1730, and most recently known as the Staples Inn, the National Historic Register building has 18 antiques-filled guest rooms with air-conditioning, phones, and TVs. Continental breakfast is included in the rates; a two-bedroom suite is $425-450.

Practically next door is **The Atlantic Birches Inn** (20 Portland Ave./Rte. 98, Old Orchard Beach, 207/934-5295 or 888/934-5295, www.atlanticbirches.com, $126-146), with 10 air-conditioned guest rooms in a

AMUSEMENT PARKS AND AMUSING PLACES

Palace Playland is a kid magnet at Old Orchard Beach.

If you've got kids or just love amusement parks, you'll find Maine's best in the Old Orchard area, where sand and sun just seem to complement arcades and rides perfectly. (All of these parks are seasonal, so call or check websites for current schedule.)

Victorian house and a separate cottage. Decor leans toward froufrou, breakfast is hearty continental, and there's a swimming pool. The beach is an easy walk. It's open all year, but call ahead off-season.

Two family-owned, beachfront motels, both with pools, have been recently renovated: **The Beachwood Motel** (29 W. Grand Ave., Old Orchard Beach, 207/934-2291, www. beachwood-motel.com, $210-265) and **The Edgewater Motor Inn** (57 W. Grand Ave., Old Orchard Beach, 800/203-2034, www. theedgewatermotorinn.com, $189-289). Both are in Old Orchard's hub, so don't expect quiet nights.

Escape the beach madness at **Hobson House Celtic Inn Bed and Breakfast** (298 Main St.,

Saco, 207/284-4113, www.hobsonhouse.com, $115-130), an elegant Federal-style mansion situated on landscaped grounds on the edge of downtown Saco. Amenities include an outdoor heated pool.

FOOD

Days and hours of operation reflect peak season and are subject to change.

Old Orchard Beach

Dining is not Old Orchard's strong point, but it is a bonanza for cheap eats. Stroll Main Street and out the pier for hot dogs, fries, pizza, and ice cream.

For casual dining, there are two choices. **Joseph's by the Sea** (55 W. Grand Ave.,

The biggie is **Funtown/Splashtown USA** (774 Portland Rd./Rte. 1, Saco, 207/284-5139 or 800/878-2900, www.funtownsplashtownusa.com). Ride Maine's only wooden roller coaster; fly down New England's longest and tallest log flume ride; free-fall 200 feet on Dragon's Descent; get wet and go wild riding speed slides, tunnel slides, raft slides, and river slides or splashing in the pool. Add a huge kiddie-ride section as well as games, food, and other activities for a full day of family fun. Ticketing options vary by the activities included and height, ranging $25-36 for "Big" (48 inches and taller), $20-27 for "Little" (38-48 inches tall) and "Senior" (over age 60), and free for kids under 38 inches tall.

Three miles north of Funtown/Splashtown USA, **Aquaboggan Water Park** (980 Portland Rd./Rte. 1, Saco, 207/282-3112, www.aquabogganwaterpark.com, 10am-6pm daily late June-Labor Day) is wet and wild, with such stomach turners as the Yankee Ripper, the Suislide, and the Stealth, with an almost-vertical drop of 45 feet—enough to accelerate to 30 mph on the descent. Wear a bathing suit that won't abandon you in the rough-and-tumble. Also, if you wear glasses, safety straps and plastic lenses are required. Besides all the water stuff, there are mini-golf, an arcade, go-karts, and bumper boats. A day pass for all pools, slides, and mini-golf is $20 (48 inches and taller), $16 (under 48 inches tall), and $5 (under 38 inches tall). Mondays are $12 general admission days. A $30 superpass also includes two go-kart rides and unlimited bumper-boat rides.

The biggest beachfront amusement park, **Palace Playland** (1 Old Orchard St., Old Orchard, 207/934-2001, www.palaceplayland.com) has more than 25 rides and attractions packed into four acres, including a giant waterslide, a fun house, bumper cars, a Ferris wheel, roller coasters, and a 24,000-square-foot arcade with more than 200 games. An unlimited pass is $32 per day; a kiddie pass good for all two-ticket rides is $24; two-day, season, and single tickets are available.

The **Old Orchard Beach's pier,** jutting 475 feet into the ocean from downtown, is a mini-mall of shops, arcades, and fast-food outlets. Far longer when it was built in 1898, it has been lopped off gradually by fires and storms. The current incarnation has been here since the late 1970s.

Old Orchard Beach, 207/934-5044, www.josephsbythesea.com, 7am-11am and 5pm-9pm daily, entrées $19-33) is a quiet shorefront restaurant amid all the hoopla. Request a table on the screened patio. The menu is heavy on seafood, but there are choices for steak lovers. A limited menu of $15 Early Bird specials is served 5pm-6pm. Reservations are advisable in midsummer.

The menu is more ambitious at **The Landmark** (28 E. Grand Ave., Old Orchard Beach, 207/934-0156, www.landmarkfinedining.com, 5pm-9pm Wed.-Sun., $18-22), where entrées, ranging from fried clams to lacquered duck, are served in a restored Victorian house; keep it simple for best results. Messy items, including lobster and ribs, are served on the patio.

Take advantage of $13.95 specials served 5pm-6pm. Children's menu available.

Camp Ellis

At **Huot's Seafood Restaurant** (Camp Ellis Beach, Saco, 207/282-1642, www.huotsseafoodrestaurant.com, 11:30am-9pm Tues.-Sun., $6-27), under third-generation management, the menu is huge, portions are large, and prices are reasonable. It's a good value for fresh seafood; children's menu available.

Saco

Craving fast-ish food? The Camire family operates Maine's best homegrown option, **Rapid Ray's** (189 Main St., 207/283-4222, www.rapidrays.biz, 11am-12:30am Mon.-Thurs.,

© TOM NANGLE

The Palace Diner is Maine's oldest diner, but the fare is updated with an emphasis on fresh and local food.

11am-1:30am Fri.-Sat., 11am-11pm Sun., $2-8). Burgers, dogs, lobster rolls, and clam cakes are served at the standing-room-only joint.

Super soups and sandwiches come from **Vic & Whits** (206 Main St., 207/284-6710, 8am-8pm Mon.-Sat., 8am-1pm Sun.), which also has a nice selection of retail wine, beer, and Maine cheeses.

Located on Saco Island in renovated factory building #3, **The Run of the Mill Public House & Brewery** (100 Main St., 207/571-9648, www.therunofthemill.net, 11:30am-9pm Sun.-Thurs., to 10pm Fri.-Sat., $8-17) is a 14-barrel brewpub with seasonal outdoor deck seating overlooking the river. Expect pub-fare classics with a few surprises.

Biddeford and Biddeford Pool

For a town grounded in Franco-American culture, Biddeford has some intriguing ethnic choices, including a few that garner praise far beyond city limits: For well-prepared Indian cuisine, seek out **Jewel of India** (26 Alfred St., 207/282-5600, www.thejewelofindia.com, 11am-10pm Tues.-Sun., entrées $13-16). If you're longing for pho and Vietnamese coffee, head into **Que Huong** (11am-8pm Mon.-Thurs., to 9pm Fri.-Sat., $7-10).

Diner fans, take note: Maine's oldest is the **Palace Diner** (18 Franklin St., Biddeford, www.palacedinerme.com, 207/284-0015, 7am-2pm Tues.-Fri., to noon Sat., $3-8), a 1926 Pollard that was towed to Maine from Lowell, Massachusetts, by horses in the same year that Lindberg flew over the Atlantic. Dine in or take it to the adjacent park. It's tucked off Main Street next to City Hall. Here's the best part: The owners are committed to using fresh, local, and organic whenever possible, making dining here not only delicious, but also healthful (as much as traditional diner fare can be healthful). Don't miss the poutine.

Dahlia's Delights (137 Main St., 207/710-2119, www.dahliasdelights.com, 11am-7pm Tues.-Sat., 10am-2pm Sun., $6-8) serves vegetarian salads, sandwiches, soups, and specials.

Buffleheads (122 Hills Beach Rd., 207/284-6000, www.buffleheadsrestaurant.com, 11:30am-2pm and 5pm-8:30pm daily, closed Mon. off-season, $8-28) is a family dining find with spectacular ocean views. Ray and Karen Wieczoreck opened the restaurant in 1994 and have built a strong local following through the years. The kids can munch on pizza, burgers, spaghetti, and other favorites while adults savor well-prepared seafood with a home-style spin or landlubber classics. Lobster pie and a turkey dinner with all the trimmings are both perennial favorites. Hills Beach Road branches off Route 9 at the University of New England campus.

Take your lobster or fried seafood dinner to an oceanfront picnic table on the grassy lawn behind **F. O. Goldthwaite's** (3 Lester B. Orcott Blvd., Biddeford Pool, 207/284-8872, 7am-7:30pm daily, $4-market rates), an old-fashioned general store. Salads, fried seafood, sandwiches, and kid-friendly fare round out the menu.

INFORMATION AND SERVICES

Sources of visitor information are **Biddeford-Saco Chamber of Commerce and Industry** (207/282-1567, www.biddefordsacochamber.org), **Old Orchard Beach Chamber of Commerce** (207/934-2500 or 800/365-9386, www.oldorchardbeachmaine.com), and **Ocean Park Association** (207/934-9068, www.oceanpark.org).

The **Dyer Library** (371 Main St., Saco, 207/282-3031, www.sacomuseum.org), next door to the Saco Museum, attracts scads of genealogists to its vast Maine history collection.

Also check out **Libby Memorial Library** (Staples St., Old Orchard Beach, 207/934-4351, www.ooblibrary.org).

GETTING THERE AND AROUND

Biddeford is about five miles or 10 minutes via Route 1 from Kennebunk. From Biddeford to Portland, it's about 18 miles or 25 minutes via I-95 and I-295; allow at least a half hour via Route 1. Downtown Biddeford is about a mile via Route 9 from downtown Saco. From Saco to Old Orchard Beach is about four miles or at least 10 minutes via Route 9, the Old Orchard Beach Road, and Route 5, but it can take twice that in summer traffic.

Amtrak's *Downeaster* (800/872-7245, www.thedowneaster.com) connects Boston's North Station with Brunswick, Maine, with stops in Wells, Saco, Old Orchard Beach (seasonal), Portland, Freeport, and Brunswick. If you're thinking day trip, take the train and avoid the traffic and parking hassles.

The **Biddeford-Saco-Old Orchard Beach Transit Committee** (207/282-5408, www.shuttlebus-zoom.com) operates three systems that make getting around simple. The **Old Orchard Beach Trolley** (10am-midnight daily late June-Labor Day) operates two routes on a regular schedule that connects restaurants and campgrounds. You can flag it down anywhere en route. Fare is $1-2 per ride; children under age five ride free. **ShuttleBus Local Service** provides frequent weekday and less-frequent weekend service (except on national holidays) between Biddeford, Saco, and Old Orchard Beach. One-way fare is $1.25 ages five and older, exact change required. **ShuttleBus InterCity Service** connects Biddeford, Saco, and Old Orchard with Portland, South Portland, and Scarborough. Fares vary by zones, topping out at $5 for anyone over age five.

GREATER PORTLAND

Whenever national magazines highlight the 10 best places to live, eat, work, or play, Greater Portland often makes the list. The very things that make the area so popular with residents make it equally attractive to visitors. Small in size but big in heart, Greater Portland entices visitors with the staples—lighthouses, lobster, and L. L. Bean—but wows them with everything else it offers. It is the state's cultural hub, with performing-arts centers, numerous festivals, and varied museums; it's also a dining destination, with nationally recognized chefs as well as an amazing assortment and variety of everyday restaurants; and despite its urban environment it has a mind-boggling number of recreational opportunities. No wonder the National Heritage Trust named it a Distinctive Destination.

Portland's population hovers around 66,000, but when the suburbs are included, it climbs to nearly 250,000, making it Maine's largest city by far. Take a swing through the bedroom communities of Scarborough (pop. 18,919), Cape Elizabeth (pop. 9,015), and South Portland (pop. 25,002), and you'll better understand the area's popularity: easily accessible parks, beaches, rocky ledges, and lighthouses all minutes from downtown along with a slew of ferry-connected islands dotting Casco Bay. Head north through suburban Falmouth (pop. 11,185) and Yarmouth (pop. 8,349), and you'll

COURTESY OF PORTLAND CONVENTION & VISITORS BUREAU

HIGHLIGHTS

LOOK FOR ◖ TO FIND RECOMMENDED SIGHTS, ACTIVITIES, DINING, AND LODGING.

◖ **The Old Port and the Waterfront:** Plan to spend at least a couple of hours browsing the shops, dining, and enjoying the energy of this restored historic district (page 66).

◖ **Portland Museum of Art (PMA):** This museum houses works by masters such as Winslow Homer, John Marin, Andrew Wyeth, Edward Hopper, and Marsden Hartley as well as works by Monet, Picasso, and Renoir (page 69).

◖ **Victoria Mansion:** This house is considered one of the most richly decorated dwellings of its period remaining in the country (page 69).

◖ **Portland Observatory:** Climb the 103 steps to the orb deck of the only remaining maritime signal tower on the eastern seaboard, and you'll be rewarded with views from the White Mountains to Casco Bay's islands (page 69).

◖ **Portland Head Light:** This lighthouse, commissioned by President George Washington, is fabulously sited on the rocky ledges of Cape Elizabeth (page 71).

◖ **Casco Bay Tour:** Take a three-hour tour on the mail boat, which stops briefly at five islands en route (page 80).

◖ **Lobstering Cruise:** Go out on a working lobster boat in Portland Harbor, see the sights, and perhaps return with a lobster for dinner (page 81).

◖ **L. L. Bean:** The empire's flagship store is in Freeport, and no trip to this shopping mecca is complete without a visit (page 98).

◖ **L.L. Bean Outdoor Discovery Schools:** Don't miss the opportunity for an inexpensive introduction to a new sport (page 101).

---

arrive in Freeport (pop. 7,879), home of megaretailer L. L. Bean. En route you'll still see the vestiges of the region's heritage: sailboats and lobster boats, traps and buoys piled on lawns or along driveways, and tucked here and there, farms with stands brimming with fresh produce.

Greater Portland also marks a transitional point on Maine's coastline. The long sand beaches of the Southern Coast begin to give way to islands and a coastline edged with a jumble of rocks and ledges spliced with rivers and coves.

It's tempting to dismiss Portland in favor of seeking the "real Maine" elsewhere along the coast, but the truth is, the real Maine is here. And although Portland alone provides plenty to keep a visitor busy, it's also an excellent base for day trips to places such as the Kennebunks, Freeport, Brunswick, and Bath, where more of that real Maine flavor awaits.

PLANNING YOUR TIME

July and August are the most popular times to visit, but Greater Portland is a year-round destination. Spring truly arrives by mid-May, when most summer outfitters begin operations at least on weekends. September is perhaps the loveliest month of the year weather-wise, and by mid-October those fabled New England maples are turning crimson.

To do the region justice, you'll want to spend at least three or four days, more if your plans call for using Greater Portland as a base for day trips to more distant points. You can easily kill two days in downtown Portland alone, what with all the shops, museums, historical sites, waterfront, and neighborhoods to explore. If you're staying in town and are an avid walker, you won't need a car to get to the in-town must-see sights.

You will need a car to reach beyond the city. Allow a full day for a leisurely tour through South Portland and Cape Elizabeth and on to Prouts Neck in Scarborough.

Rabid shoppers should either stay in Freeport or allow at least a day for L. L. Bean and the 100 or so outlets in its shadow. If you're traveling with a supershopper, don't despair. Freeport has parks and preserves that are light-years removed from the frenzy of its downtown, and the fishing village of South Freeport offers seaworthy pleasures.

HISTORY

Portland's downtown, a crooked-finger peninsula projecting into Casco Bay and today defined vaguely by I-295 at its "knuckle," was named Machigonne (Great Neck) by the Wabanaki, the Native Americans who held sway when English settlers first arrived in 1632. Characteristically, the Brits renamed the region Falmouth (it included present-day Falmouth, Portland, South Portland, Westbrook, and Cape Elizabeth) and the peninsula Falmouth Neck, but it was 130 years before they secured real control of the area. Anglo-French squabbles spurred by the governments' conflicts in Europe drew in the Wabanaki from Massachusetts to Nova Scotia. Falmouth was only one of the battlegrounds, and it was a fairly minor one. Relative calm resumed in the 1760s only to be broken by the stirrings of rebellion centered on Boston. When Falmouth's citizens expressed support for the incipient revolution, the punishment was a 1775 naval onslaught that wiped out 75 percent of the houses, which created a decade-long setback. In 1786, Falmouth Neck became Portland, a thriving trading community where shipping flourished until the 1807 imposition of the Embargo Act. Severing trade and effectively shutting down Portland Harbor for a year and a half, the legislation did more harm to the fledgling colonies of the United States than to the French and British it was designed to punish.

In 1820, when Maine became a state, Portland was named its capital. The city became a crucial transportation hub with the arrival of the railroad. The Civil War was barely a blip in Portland's history, but the year after it ended, the city suffered a devastating blow: Exuberant Fourth of July festivities in 1866 sparked a conflagration that virtually leveled the city. The Great Fire spared only the Portland Observatory and a chunk of the West End. Evidence of the city's Victorian rebirth remains today in many downtown neighborhoods.

After World War II, Portland slipped into decline for several years, but that is over. The city's waterfront revival began in the 1970s and continues today, despite commercial competition from South Portland's Maine Mall. Congress Street has blossomed as an arts and retail district, public green space is increasing, and an influx of immigrants is changing the city's cultural makeup. With the new century, Portland is on a roll.

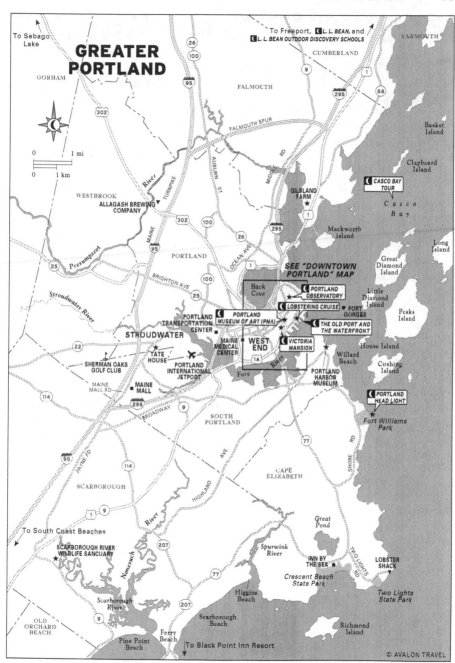

GREATER PORTLAND

GREATER PORTLAND

To Sebago
Lake

GORHAM

To Freeport, **L. L. BEAN**, and
L. L. BEAN OUTDOOR DISCOVERY SCHOOLS

YARMOUTH

CUMBERLAND

FALMOUTH

FALMOUTH SPUR

Basket
Island

Clapboard
Island

WESTBROOK
ALLAGASH BREWING
COMPANY

CASCO BAY
TOUR

Casco
Bay

Mackworth
Island

Long
Island

Stroudwater River

PORTLAND

SEE "DOWNTOWN
PORTLAND" MAP

Great
Diamond
Island

Back
Cove

PORTLAND
OBSERVATORY

Little
Diamond
Island

Peaks
Island

STROUDWATER

PORTLAND
TRANSPORTATION
CENTER

PORTLAND
MUSEUM OF ART (PMA)

LOBSTERING CRUISE

FORT
GORGES

THE OLD PORT AND
THE WATERFRONT

MAINE
MEDICAL
CENTER

WEST
END

VICTORIA
MANSION

House Island

SHERMAN OAKS
GOLF CLUB

TATE
HOUSE

Willard
Beach

Cushing
Island

PORTLAND
INTERNATIONAL
JETPORT

Fort

PORTLAND
HARBOR
MUSEUM

MAINE
MALL RD

MAINE
MALL

PORTLAND
HEAD LIGHT

BROADWAY

SOUTH
PORTLAND

Fort Williams
Park

SCARBOROUGH

CAPE
ELIZABETH

To South Coast Beaches

Great
Pond

SCARBOROUGH RIVER
WILDLIFE SANCUARY

Spurwink
River

INN BY
THE SEA

LOBSTER
SHACK

Crescent Beach
State Park

Scarborough
River

Higgins
Beach

Two Lights
State Park

OLD
ORCHARD
BEACH

Scarborough
Beach

Richmond
Island

Pine Point
Beach

Ferry
Beach

To Black Point Inn Resort

GILSLAND
FARM

0   1 mi
0   1 km

© AVALON TRAVEL

Portland

Often compared to San Francisco (an oft-cited but never verified statistic boasts that it vies with San Francisco for the title of most restaurants per capita), Portland is small, friendly, and easily explored on foot, although at times it may seem that no matter which direction you head, it's uphill. The heart of Portland is the peninsula jutting into Casco Bay. Bordering that are the Eastern and Western Promenades, Back Cove, and the working waterfront. Salty sea breezes cool summer days and make winter ones seem even chillier. Unlike that other city by the bay, snow frequently blankets Portland December-March.

Portland is Maine's most ethnically diverse city, with active refugee resettlement programs and dozens of languages spoken in the schools. Although salty sailors can still be found along the waterfront, Portland is increasingly a professional community with young, upwardly mobile residents spiffing up Victorian houses and infusing new energy and money into the city's neighborhoods.

The region's cultural hub, Portland has world-class museums and performing-arts centers, active historical and preservation groups, an art school and a university, a symphony orchestra, numerous galleries and coffeehouses, and enough activities to keep culture vultures busy well into the night, especially in the thriving, handsomely restored Old Port and the up-and-coming Arts District.

Portland is also a playground for sports- and outdoors-lovers, with trails for running, biking, skating, and cross-country skiing, water sports aplenty, and a beloved minor-league baseball team, the Sea Dogs. When city folks want to escape, they often hop a ferry for one of the islands of Casco Bay or head to one of the parks, preserves, or beaches in the suburbs.

Still, Portland remains a major seaport.

Lobster boats, commercial fishing vessels, long-distance passenger boats, cruise ships, and local ferries dominate the working waterfront, and the briny scent of the sea—or bait—seasons the air.

PORTLAND NEIGHBORHOODS

The best way to appreciate the character of Portland's neighborhoods is on foot. So much of Portland can (and should) be covered on foot that it would take a whole book to list all the possibilities, but several dedicated volunteer groups have produced guides to facilitate the process.

Greater Portland Landmarks (207/774-5561, www.portlandlandmarks.org) is the doyenne, founded in 1964 to preserve Portland's historic architecture and promote responsible construction. The organization has published more than a dozen books and booklets, including *Discover Historic Portland on Foot,* a packet of four well-researched walking-tour guides to architecturally historic sections of Portland's peninsula: Old Port, Western Promenade, State Street, and Congress Street. It's available online or for $6 at local bookstores, some gift shops, and the Visitor Information Center (14 Ocean Gateway Pier, 207/772-5800). Ask about guided walking tours highlighting neighborhoods or sights. Self-guided tours can be downloaded from the Landmarks website.

◖ The Old Port and the Waterfront

Tony shops, cobblestone sidewalks, replica streetlights, and a casual upmarket crowd (most of the time) set the scene for a district once filled with derelict buildings. Scores of boutiques, enticing restaurants, and spontaneous street-corner music make it a fun area to visit year-round. Nightlife centers on the Old Port,

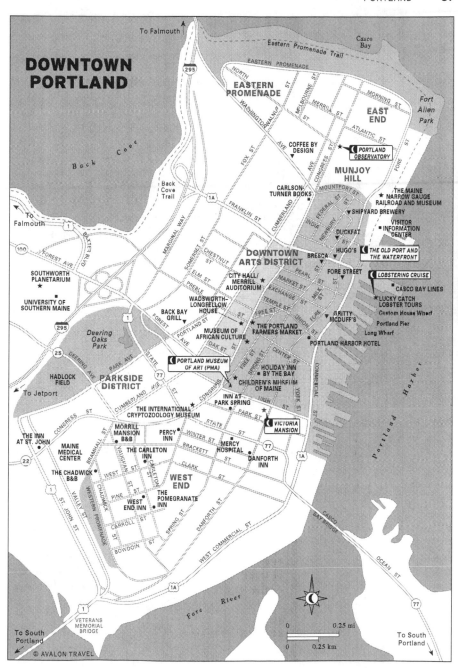

GREATER PORTLAND

DOWNTOWN PORTLAND

To Falmouth

Casco Bay

Eastern Promenade Trail

EASTERN PROMENADE

NORTH

295

EASTERN PROMENADE

MORNING ST

Fort Allen Park

EAST END

ATLANTIC ST

★ PORTLAND OBSERVATORY

COFFEE BY DESIGN

MUNJOY HILL

Back Cove Trail

CARLSON-TURNER BOOKS

★ THE MAINE NARROW GAUGE RAILROAD AND MUSEUM

1A

FRANKLIN ST

▼ SHIPYARD BREWERY

To Falmouth

1

DUCKFAT

VISITOR INFORMATION CENTER

100

FOREST AVE

HUGO'S

THE OLD PORT AND THE WATERFRONT

BRESCA

DOWNTOWN ARTS DISTRICT

FORE STREET

LOBSTERING CRUISE

SOUTHWORTH PLANETARIUM ★

CITY HALL/ MERRILL AUDITORIUM ★

CASCO BAY LINES

★ LUCKY CATCH LOBSTER TOURS

UNIVERSITY OF SOUTHERN MAINE

WADSWORTH-LONGFELLOW HOUSE

Custom House Wharf

BACK BAY GRILL ▼

Portland Pier

295

Deering Oaks Park

MUSEUM OF AFRICAN CULTURE

★ THE PORTLAND FARMERS MARKET

GRITTY McDUFF'S ▼

Long Wharf

25

PORTLAND HARBOR HOTEL

PORTLAND MUSEUM OF ART (PMA)

HADLOCK FIELD

PARKSIDE DISTRICT

77

HOLIDAY INN BY THE BAY

CHILDREN'S MUSEUM OF MAINE

To Jetport

INN AT PARK SPRING

Portland Harbor

THE INTERNATIONAL CRYPTOZOOLOGY MUSEUM

VICTORIA MANSION

THE INN AT ST. JOHN

MORRILL MANSION B&B

PERCY INN

MERCY HOSPITAL

22

MAINE MEDICAL CENTER

THE CARLETON INN

DANFORTH INN

1A

THE CHADWICK B&B

WEST END

1

THE POMEGRANATE INN

WEST END INN

CASCO BAY BRIDGE

To South Portland

1

VETERANS MEMORIAL BRIDGE

Fore River

OCEAN ST

77

To South Portland

0   0.25 mi

0   0.25 km

© AVALON TRAVEL

© HILARY NANGLE

The Old Port

and a few dozen bars keep everyone hopping until after midnight. Police keep a close eye on the district, but it can get a bit dicey after 11pm on weekends.

Congress Street and the Downtown Arts District

Bit by bit, once-declining Congress Street is being revitalized, showcasing the best of the city's culture. Galleries, artists' studios, coffeehouses, cafés, and bistros as well as libraries, museums, and performing-arts centers are all part of the ongoing renaissance.

West End

Probably the most diverse of the city's downtown neighborhoods, and one that largely escaped the Great Fire of 1866, the West End includes the historically and architecturally splendid Western Promenade, Maine Medical Center (the state's largest hospital), the city's best bed-and-breakfasts, a gay-friendly

community with a laissez-faire attitude, and a host of cafés and restaurants as well as a few niches harboring the homeless and forlorn.

Munjoy Hill and the East End

A once slightly down-at-the-heels neighborhood enclave with a pull-'em-up-by-the-bootstraps attitude, Portland's East End is rapidly gentrifying. Munjoy Hill is probably best known for the distinctive wooden tower crowning its summit.

Named for George Munjoy, a wealthy 17th-century resident, this district has a host of architectural and historic landmarks, making it well worth a walking tour. Fortunately, Greater Portland Landmarks (207/774-5561, www.portlandlandmarks.org) has produced a 24-page booklet, *Munjoy Hill Historic Guide* ($3), which documents more than 60 notable sites, including the Eastern Cemetery, which is on the National Register of Historic Places, and the Eastern Promenade and Fort Allen Park, with spectacular harbor views.

Bayside and Parkside

A Babel of languages reverberates in these districts just below Portland City Hall. Bayside experienced the arrival of refugees—Cambodian, Laotian, Vietnamese, Central European, and Afghan families—from war-torn lands during the 1980s and 1990s. Nowadays you'll hear references to Somali Town, an area named for all the resettled refugees from that shattered country. Others have come from Sudan and Ethiopia. Portland's active Refugee Resettlement Program has assisted all of them, and many newcomers have become entrepreneurs, opening restaurants and small markets catering to their compatriots but increasingly gaining customers among other residents.

Stroudwater

Off the downtown peninsula at the western

edge of Portland, close to the Portland Jetport, is the historic area known as Stroudwater, once an essential link in Maine water transport. The 20-mile-long **Cumberland and Oxford Canal,** hand-dug in 1828, ran through here as part of the timber-shipping route linking Portland Harbor, the Fore and Presumpscot Rivers, and Sebago Lake. Twenty-eight wooden locks allowed vessels to rise the 265 feet between sea level and the lake. By 1870 trains took over the route, condemning the canal to oblivion. The centerpiece of the Stroudwater area today is the historic 18th-century Tate House.

SIGHTS
◖ Portland Museum of Art (PMA)

Three centuries of art and architecture can be discovered at Maine's oldest (since 1882) and finest art museum, the Portland Museum of Art (7 Congress Sq., 207/775-6148, recorded info 207/773-2787 or 800/639-4067, www. portlandmuseum.org, 10am-5pm Sat.-Sun. and Tues.-Thurs., 10am-9pm Fri., closed Mon. mid-Oct.-late May, $12 adults, $10 seniors and students, $6 ages 6-17, free 5pm-9pm every Fri.). The museum's topflight collection of American and impressionist masters and fine and decorative arts is displayed in three architecturally stunning connected buildings: the award-winning Charles Shipman Payson building, designed by I. M. Pei and opened in 1983; the newly restored Federal-era McLellan House; and the Beaux-Arts L. D. M. Sweat Memorial Galleries, designed by noted Maine architect John Calvin Stevens. The museum also has a well-stocked gift shop and a pleasant café that's open for lunch daily (11am-4pm) and dinner Friday until 7:30pm. Check the website for current family activities, lectures, and other events, including **Movies at the Museum** ($7), showcasing foreign, classical, and art films.

◖ Victoria Mansion

The jaws of first-time visitors literally drop when they enter the Italianate Victoria Mansion (109 Danforth St., 207/772-4841, www.victoriamansion.org, 10am-4pm Mon.-Sat., 1pm-5pm Sun. May-Oct., special hours in Dec., $15 adults, $13.50 seniors, $5 children 6-17, $35 family, no senior discount in holiday season), also called the Morse-Libby Mansion. It's widely considered the most magnificently ornamented dwelling of its period remaining in the country. The National Historic Landmark is rife with Victoriana: carved marble fireplaces, elaborate porcelain and paneling, a freestanding mahogany staircase, gilded glass chandeliers, a restored 6-by-25-foot stained-glass ceiling window, and unbelievable trompe l'oeil touches. It's even more spectacular at Christmas, with yards of roping, festooned trees, and carolers; this is the best time to bring kids, as the house itself may not particularly intrigue them. The mansion was built in the late 1850s by Ruggles Sylvester Morse, a Maine-born entrepreneur whose New Orleans-based fortune enabled him to hire 93 craftspeople to complete the house. The interior, designed by Gustave Herter, still boasts 90 percent of the original furnishings. Guided 45-minute tours begin every half hour on the quarter hour in season; tours are self-guided during the holidays.

◖ Portland Observatory

Providing a head-swiveling view of Portland (and the White Mountains on a clear day), the octagonal red-painted Portland Observatory (138 Congress St., 207/774-5561, www.portlandlandmarks.org, 10am-5pm daily late May-mid-Oct., last tour at 4:30pm, sunset tours 5pm-8pm Thurs. July-Aug., $8 adults, $5 children 6-16) is the only remaining marine signal tower on the eastern seaboard. Built in 1807 at a cost of $5,000 by Captain Lemuel Moody to keep track of the port's shipping activity, the tower has 122 tons of rock ballast

Longfellow Square honors poet Henry Wadsworth Longfellow, who spent his boyhood in Portland.

in its base. Admission in those days (only men were allowed to climb the 103 interior steps) was 12.5 cents. Today, admission includes the small museum at the tower's base and a guided tour to the top.

The Longfellow Connection

A few blocks down Congress Street from the PMA you can step back in time to the era of Portland-born poet Henry Wadsworth Longfellow, who lived in the accurately re-stored **Wadsworth-Longfellow House** (485 Congress St., 207/774-1822, www.mainehistory.org, 10am-5pm Mon.-Sat., noon-5pm Sun. May 1-Oct. 31, last tour 4pm, special holiday hours Nov.-Dec., $12 adults, $10 seniors and students, $3 ages 5-17) as a child in the early 1800s, long before the brick mansion was dwarfed by surrounding high-rises. Wadsworth and Longfellow family furnishings

fill the three-story house, owned by the Maine Historical Society, and savvy guides provide insight into Portland's 19th-century life. Don't miss the urban oasis—a wonderfully peaceful garden—behind the house (same hours, free). Buy tickets at the adjacent Center for Maine History, which also houses the **Maine History Gallery** ($8 adults, $7 seniors, $2 children), where you can take in the Maine Historical Society's current exhibits and find an extensive collection of Maine history books in the gift shop.

Maine Narrow Gauge Railroad and Museum

A three-mile ride along Portland's waterfront is the highlight of a visit to the Maine Narrow Gauge Railroad Company and Museum (58 Fore St., 207/828-0814, www.mngrr.org). The museum (10am-4pm daily late May-late Oct., 10am-4pm Mon.-Fri. off-season, $3 adults, $2 seniors and ages 3-12, free with train ticket) owns more than three dozen train cars and has others on long-term loan, most from Maine's five historic narrow-gauge railroads, the last of which closed in 1943. You can board a number of the cars and see others undergoing restoration. For a fee you can ride the two-foot rails aboard a multicar train. The schedule roughly follows museum hours, with rides on the hour ($10 adults, $9 seniors, $6 ages 3-12). The track edges Casco Bay along the Eastern Promenade; it's a short but enjoyable excursion that's a real kid pleaser.

Museum of African Culture

Here's a little treasure: Founded in 1998, the Museum of African Culture (13 Brown St., 207/871-7188, www.museumafricanculture. org, 10:30am-4pm Tues.-Fri., noon-4pm Sat., $5 suggested donation) is the brainchild of Nigerian-born Oscar Mokeme (the director) and Arthur Aleshire. It's devoted to sub-Saharan African arts and culture. Among the

© HILARY NANGLE

museum's 1,500 or so treasures—not all on display at once—are Nigerian tribal masks and Beninese lost-wax bronzes.

Children's Museum of Maine

Here's the answer to parents' prayers: a whole museum in downtown Portland catering to kids. At the Children's Museum of Maine (142 Free St., 207/828-1234, www.kitetails.com, 10am-5pm Mon.-Sat., noon-5pm Sun. late May-early Sept., 10am-5pm Tues.-Sat., noon-5pm Sun. early Sept.-late May, $9, free for children under 18 months, $1 admission 5pm-8pm first Fri. of each month) lots of hands-on exhibits encourage interaction and guarantee involvement for a couple of hours. Guided tours of the Camera Obscura exhibit are $4.

The International Cryptozoology Museum

An eight-foot-tall likeness of a bigfoot greets visitors at former university professor and author Loren Coleman's cryptozoology museum (11 Avon St., 207/518-9496, www.cryptozoologymuseum.com, noon-4pm Mon., 11am-8pm Wed.-Sat., noon-3:30pm Sun., call to confirm hours, $7). Coleman is a renowned expert in cryptozoology, the story of hidden animals such as bigfoot, the Loch Ness monster, and the abominable snowman. He has amassed a collection of artifacts such as skulls and footprint castings that lend credence to the existence of these rumored beasts, as well as kitsch that includes movie props and souvenir memorabilia. This is always a big hit with kids.

Brewery Tours

Look for the keg topping the flagpole at **Shipyard Brewery** (86 Newbury St., 207/761-0807, www.shipyard.com). Full brewery tours are offered on Tuesday evenings; make reservations well in advance. Free, one-hour tours with sampling at **Allagash Brewing Company** (50 Industrial Way, 207/878-5385,

www.allagash.com) are by online reservation. **Geary's Brewing Company** (38 Evergreen Dr., 207/878-2337, www.gearybrewing.com) offers tours by appointment.

Southworth Planetarium

Under a 30-foot dome with comfy theater seats and a state-of-the-art laser system, the Southworth Planetarium (Science Building, University of Southern Maine, 70 Falmouth St., 207/780-4249, www.usm.maine.edu/planet) presents astronomy shows, with ticket prices around $6. Take Exit 6B off I-295 and go west on Forest Avenue to Falmouth Street (a left turn). The Science Building is on the left past the parking lot.

Tate House

Just down the street from the Portland International Jetport, in the Stroudwater district, is the 1755 Tate House (1270 Westbrook St., 207/774-6177, tatehouse.org, 10am-4pm Wed.-Sat., 1pm-4pm Sun., last tour 3pm, mid-June-mid-Oct., $8 adults, $6 seniors, $3 ages 6-12), a National Historic Landmark owned by the Colonial Dames of America. Built by Captain George Tate, who was prominent in shipbuilding, the house overlooks the Stroudwater River and has superb period furnishings and a lovely 18th-century herb garden with more than 70 species. Tours last 40 minutes. Cellar-to-attic tours are offered twice weekly, $10 adults, $8 seniors, $6 children.

◖ Portland Head Light

Just four miles from downtown Portland in Cape Elizabeth, Fort Williams feels a world away. This oceanfront town park, a former military base, is home to Portland Head Light (1000 Shore Rd., Cape Elizabeth, 207/799-2661, www.portlandheadlight.com, dawn-dusk daily). Commissioned by President George Washington and first lighted in 1791, it has been immortalized in poetry,

LIGHTHOUSES AND PARKS TOUR

Whether in a car or on a bike, it's easy to loop through South Portland and Cape Elizabeth on a route that takes in lighthouses, forts, beaches, and parks.

Begin just over the Casco Bay Bridge from downtown Portland on Route 77, take Broadway, and continue to the end at **Southern Maine Community College (SMCC),** overlooking the bay. The best time to come here is evenings and weekends, when there's ample parking. Unless it's foggy (when the signal is deafening) or thundering (when you'll expose yourself to lightning), walk out along the 1,000-foot granite breakwater to the **Spring Point Ledge Light** (207/699-2676, www.spring-pointlight.org), with fabulous views in every direction. Volunteers usually open it 11am-3pm Sat.-Sun., July-early Sept., $5. Also here are picnic benches, the remains of Fort Preble, and the **Spring Point Shoreline Walkway,** a scenic three-mile path with views to House, Peaks, and Cushings Islands. At the end of the path you'll reach crescent-shaped **Willard Beach,** a neighborhood place with restrooms, a snack bar, and those same marvelous views.

From the SMCC campus, return on Broadway to the major intersection with Cottage Road and bear left. Cottage Road becomes Shore Road at the Cape Elizabeth town line. Loop into Fort Williams Park and make a pilgrimage to **Portland Head Light** before continuing on Shore Road to its intersection with Route 77. Bear left, follow it to Two Lights Road, and follow the signs to 40-acre **Two Lights State Park.** Almost a pocket park, it has picnicking and restroom facilities, but its biggest asset is the panoramic ocean view from atop a onetime gun battery. Summer admission is $4.50 nonresident adults, $3 Maine resident adults, $1.50 nonresident seniors, $1 ages 5-11.

Before or after visiting the park, continue on Two Lights Road to the parking lot at the end, where you'll see the signal towers for which Two Lights is named. There's no access to either, and only one still works. If you haven't brought a picnic for the state park, there are few places finer to enjoy the view and a lobster than at **The Lobster Shack.**

To get some beach time, return to Route 77 and continue to **Crescent Beach State Park,** a 243-acre park with changing rooms, a lifeguard, restrooms, picnic tables, and a snack bar. Admission is $6.50 nonresident adults, $4.50 Maine resident adults, $1.50 senior nonresidents, $1 ages 5-11. Directly offshore is **Richmond Island,** a 200-acre private preserve with a checkered past dating to the 17th century.

---

photography, and philately. The surf here is awesome—perhaps too awesome, as the *Annie C. Maguire* was shipwrecked below the lighthouse on Christmas Eve 1886. There's no access to the 58-foot automated light tower, but the restored keeper's house has become **The Museum at Portland Head Light** (10am-4pm daily late May-Oct. 31, 10am-4pm Sat.-Sun. late spring and late fall, call to confirm dates, $2 adults, $1 ages 6-18). It's filled with local history and lighthouse memorabilia. The 90-acre oceanfront park offers much more to explore, including ruins of the fort and the Goddard mansion. Walk the trails, play a game of tennis, or dip your toes into the surf at the rocky beach. Warning: There's a strong undertow here. The grassy headlands are great places to watch the boat traffic going in and out of Portland Harbor. Bring a picnic lunch, and don't forget a kite. From downtown Portland, take Route 77 and then Broadway, Cottage Road, and Shore Road; the route is marked.

ENTERTAINMENT AND EVENTS

The best places to find out what's playing at area theaters, cinemas, concert halls, and nightclubs are the *Portland Phoenix* (www.portlandphoenix.com) and the *Go*

COURTESY OF PORTLAND CONVENTION & VISITORS BUREAU

GREATER PORTLAND

Portland Head Light

supplement in the Thursday edition of the *Portland Press Herald* (www.mainetoday.com). Both have online listings; hard copies are available at bookstores and supermarkets. The *Phoenix* is free.

Nightlife
LIVE MUSIC
The Portland Conservatory of Music presents free weekly **Noonday Concerts** at First Parish Church (425 Congress St., 207/773-5747, www.portlandconservatory.net) at 12:15pm most Thursdays October-early April. The music varies widely—perhaps jazz, classical, or choral.

Portland Parks and Recreation sponsors **Summer in the Parks** (207/756-8275, www.portlandmaine.gov/rec/summer.htm, July-Aug., free), a number of evening concert series and a midday kids' performance series in downtown parks.

In summer, take the ferry to Peaks Island for Reggae Sundays on the deck at **Jones Landing** (at the ferry landing, Peaks Island, 207/766-4400); doors open at 11:30am.

BREWPUBS AND BARS
Portland is a beer town, with an ever-increasing number of microbreweries and brewpubs. It's also vigilant about enforcing alcohol laws, so even if you're well older than 21, be sure to bring valid identification. Bars close at 1am.

Not only is **Gritty McDuff's** (396 Fore St., Old Port, 207/772-2739) one of Maine's most popular breweries, but its brewpub was the state's first—opened in 1988. The menu includes pub classics such as fish-and-chips and shepherd's pie as well as burgers, salads, and sandwiches. Gritty's also books live entertainment fairly regularly. Tours are available by appointment. Gritty's also has a branch in Freeport.

A longtime favorite pub, **$3 Dewey's** (241

Commercial St., Old Port, 207/772-3310, www.threedollardeweys.com) is so authentic that visiting Brits, Kiwis, and Aussies often head here to assuage their homesickness. Inexpensive fare, 36 brews on tap, free popcorn, and frequent live music make it a very popular spot.

Especially popular in the late afternoon and early evening is **J's Oyster** (5 Portland Pier, 207/772-4828), a longtime fixture (some might call it a dive) on the waterfront known for its raw bar and for pouring a good drink.

Of all Portland's neighborhood hangouts, **Ruski's** (212 Danforth St., 207/774-7604) is the most authentic—a small, usually crowded onetime speakeasy that rates just as highly for breakfast as for nighttime schmoozing. Expect basic homemade fare for well under $10, plus darts and a big-screen TV. Dress down or you'll feel out of place.

Other dress-down neighborhood bars are **Rosie's** (330 Fore St., 207/772-5656), **Mama's Crowbar** (189 Congress St., 207/357-7678), and **Blackstones** (6 Pine St., 207/775-2885, www.blackstones.com), which claims to be Portland's oldest neighborhood gay bar.

Novare Res Bier Cafe (4 Canal Plaza, 207/761-2437, www.novareresbiercafe.com) carries nearly 500 bottled beers from around the world and has 32 rotating taps. Pair them with selections from the meat-and-cheese bar, sandwiches, or small plates.

West of I-295, **The Great Lost Bear** (540 Forest Ave., 207/772-0300, www.greatlostbear.com) has 69 brews on tap, representing 15 Maine microbreweries and 50 others from the Northeast. The bear motif and the punny menus are a bit much, but the 15 or so varieties of burgers are not bad. It's a kid pleaser.

For more upscale tippling, head for **Gingko Blue** (455 Fore St., 207/541-9190, www.gingkoblue.com), with some of the city's top mixologists.

BARS WITH ENTERTAINMENT

There are so many possibilities in this category that the best advice is to scope out the scene when you arrive; the *Portland Phoenix* has the best listings. Most clubs have cover charges. The coolest venue with the hottest acts is **Port City Music Hall** (504 Congress St., 207/899-4990, www.portcitymusichall.com), a three-floor entertainment emporium. **Asylum** (121 Center St., 207/772-8274, www.portlandasylum.com) caters to a young crowd with dance jams, CD release parties, DJ nights, and live bands. **Geno's** (625 Congress St., 207/221-2382) has been at it for years—an old reliable for rock music with an emphasis on local bands. Ever popular for its Wednesday Rap Night hip-hop and weekend bands is **The Big Easy** (55 Market St., 207/871-8817, www.bigeasyportland.com). **Blue** (650A Congress St., 207/774-4111, www.portcityblue.com) presents local artists and musicians in a small space and serves beer, wine, tea, and light fare; traditional Irish music is always featured on Wednesday evening, and jazz on Saturday. Wanna rock? See what's on the calendar at **Empire Dine and Dance** (575 Congress St., 207/879-8988, www.portlandempire.com), where the entertainment includes live music and CD release parties upstairs as well as daily entertainment ranging from bluegrass to jazz downstairs.

Performing Arts

MERRILL AUDITORIUM

The magnificently restored Merrill Auditorium (20 Myrtle St., box office 207/874-8200, www.porttix.com) is a 1,900-seat theater inside Portland City Hall on Congress Street with two balconies and one of the country's only municipally owned pipe organs, the **Kotzschmar Organ** (207/553-4363, www.foko.org), under repair and not returning to the stage until 2014.

Special events and concerts are common at Merrill, and the auditorium is also home to a number of the city's arts organizations. The **Portland Symphony Orchestra** (207/842-0800, portlandsymphony.org) and presenting organization **Portland Ovations** (207/773-3150, www.portlandovations.org) have extensive, well-patronized fall and winter schedules; the PSO presents three summer Independence Pops concerts as well. The **Portland Opera Repertory Theatre** (207/879-7678, www.portopera.org) performs a major opera each summer. In addition there are films, lectures, and other related events throughout July.

Tickets for these organizations are available through PortTix (207/942-0800, www.porttix.com).

ONE LONGFELLOW SQUARE

Diverse programming is the hallmark of One Longfellow Square (207/761-1757, www.onelongfellowsquare.com), an intimate venue for performances and lectures at the corner of Congress and State Streets.

STATE THEATER

The State (609 Congress St., 207/956-6000, www.statetheatreportland.com), built in 1929 with Art Deco, Spanish, and Italian decor elements, hosts national touring artists as well as up-and-comers.

PORTLAND STAGE COMPANY

Innovative staging and controversial contemporary dramas are typical of the Portland Stage Company (Portland Performing Arts Center, 25A Forest Ave., 207/774-0465, www.portlandstage.org), established in 1974 and going strong ever since. Equity pros present a half-dozen plays each winter season in a 290-seat performance space.

Events

Summer brings plentiful events, including the **Old Port Festival,** one of the city's largest festivals, usually the first weekend of June.

It has entertainment, food and craft booths, and impromptu fun in Portland's Old Port. The **Greek Heritage Festival,** usually the last weekend of June, features Greek food, dancing, and crafts at Holy Trinity Church (133 Pleasant St.).

Some of the world's top runners join upward of 500 racers in the **Beach to Beacon Race,** held in late July-early August. The 10K course goes from Crescent Beach State Park to Portland Head Light in Cape Elizabeth.

In mid-August the **Italian Street Festival** showcases music, Italian food, and games at St. Peter's Catholic Church (72 Federal St.). Artists from all over the country set up in 350 booths along Congress Street for the annual **Sidewalk Arts Festival** in late August.

The big October wing-ding is the **Harvest on the Harbor,** a celebration of all things food- and wine-related with tastings, dinners, exhibits, and special events.

The **Maine Brewers' Festival,** the first weekend in November at the Portland Exposition Building, is a big event that expands every year thanks to the explosion of Maine microbreweries; there are samples galore. From Thanksgiving weekend to Christmas Eve, **Victorian Holiday** in downtown Portland harks back with caroling, special sales, concerts, tree lighting, horse-drawn wagons, and Victoria Mansion tours and festivities.

SHOPPING

The Portland peninsula is thick with non-cookie-cutter shops and galleries. The Old Port/Waterfront and Arts District have the highest concentration, but more and more are opening on the East End. These listings offer just a taste to spur your explorations.

Bookstores

Longfellow Books (1 Monument Way, 207/772-4045) sells new and used books and hosts readings. **Carlson-Turner Books** (241

© HILARY NANGLE

The renovated Victorian buildings of the Old Port and Waterfront are filled with independent shops.

Congress St., 207/773-4200 or 800/540-7323), on Munjoy Hill, has an extensive used-book inventory.

Art Galleries

Portland has dozens upon dozens of studios and galleries. A great way to discover them is on the **First Friday Artwalk** (www.firstfridayart-walk.com) on the first Friday evening of each month, when intown galleries host exhibition openings, open houses, meet-the-artist gatherings, and other artsy activities.

Galleries specializing in contemporary art include **June Fitzpatrick Gallery** (112 High St., 522 Congress St., 207/699-5083, www.junefitzpatrickgallery.com), **Aucocisco** (89 Exchange St., 207/553-2222, www.aucocisco.com), specializing in contemporary fine art, and **Greenhut Galleries** (146 Middle St., 207/772-2693, www.greenhutgalleries.com),

specializing in contemporary Maine art and sculpture. More than 15 Maine potters—with a wide variety of styles and items—market their wares at the **Maine Potters Market** (376 Fore St., 207/774-1633, www.mainepottersmarket.com).

Specialty Shops

Check out the latest home accessories from Maine-based designer **Angela Adams** (273 Congress St., 207/774-3523).

Woof: The company outlet **Planet Dog** (211 Marginal Way, 207/347-8606, www.planet-dog.com) is a howling good time for dogs and their owners. You'll find all sorts of wonderful products, and Planet Dog, whose motto is to "think globally and act doggedly," has established a foundation to promote and serve causes such as dog therapy, service, search and rescue, bomb sniffing, and police dogs.

Ferdinand (243 Congress St., 207/761-2151) is chock full of eclectic finds, including screen prints, jewelry, vintage clothing, and cards created on the owners letterpress. Cool place.

The stained-glass artwork is irresistible at **Laura Fuller Design Studio** (129 Congress St., 207/650-6989).

Follow your nose into **2 Note Botanical Perfumery** (97 Exchange St., 207/838-2815) for handcrafted, all-natural perfumes and bath and body product.

RECREATION
Parks, Preserves, and Beaches

Take precautions against disease-carrying mosquitoes and ticks when exploring preserves. Greater Portland is blessed with green space, thanks largely to the efforts of 19th-century mayor James Phinney Baxter, who had the foresight to hire the famed Olmsted Brothers to develop an ambitious plan to ring the city with public parks and promenades. Not all the elements fell into place, but the result is what makes Portland such a livable city.

TRAIL NETWORK

Portland Trails (305 Commercial St., 207/775-2411, www.trails.org), a dynamic membership conservation organization incorporated in 1991, is dedicated to creating and maintaining a 50-mile network of hiking and biking trails in Greater Portland. It already has 31 mapped trails to its credit, including the 2.1-mile Eastern Promenade Trail, a landscaped bay-front dual pathway circling the base of Munjoy Hill and linking East End Beach to the Old Port, and a continuing trail connecting the Eastern Prom with the 3.5-mile Back Cove Trail, on the other side of I-295. Trail maps are available on the website. The group also holds organized walks ($5 nonmembers)—a great way to meet some locals. Better still, join Portland Trails ($35 per year) and support its ambitious efforts.

DOWNTOWN PENINSULA

Probably the most visible of the city's parks, 51-acre **Deering Oaks** (Park Ave. between Forest Ave. and Deering Ave.) is best known for the quaint little duck condo in the middle of the pond. Other facilities and highlights here are tennis courts, a playground, horseshoes, rental paddleboats, a snack bar, the award-winning Rose Circle, a farmers market (7am–noon Sat.), and, in winter, ice skating. After dark, steer clear of the park.

At one end of the Eastern Promenade, where it meets Fore Street, **Fort Allen Park** overlooks offshore Fort Gorges (coin-operated telescopes bring it closer). A central gazebo is flanked by an assortment of military souvenirs dating as far back as the War of 1812. All along the Eastern Prom are walking paths, benches, play areas, and even an ill-maintained fitness trail—all with that terrific view. Down by the water is **East End Beach,** with parking, token sand, and the area's best launching ramp for sea kayaks or powerboats.

WEST OF THE DOWNTOWN PENINSULA

Just beyond I-295 along Baxter Boulevard (Rte. 1) and tidal **Back Cove** is a skinny green strip with a 3.5-mile trail for walking, jogging, or just watching the sailboards and the skyline. Along the way, you can cross Baxter Boulevard and spend time picnicking, playing tennis, or flying a kite in 48-acre **Payson Park.**

Talk about an urban oasis. The 85-acre **Fore River Sanctuary** (sunrise to sunset daily), managed by Portland Trails, has two miles of blue-blazed trails that wind through a salt marsh, link with the historic Cumberland and Oxford Canal towpath, and pass near **Jewell Falls,** Portland's only waterfall, protected by Portland Trails. From downtown Portland, take Congress Street West (Rte. 22) past I-295 to the Maine Orthopedic Center parking lot at the corner of Frost; park in the far corner.

Bird-watchers flock to 239-acre **Evergreen Cemetery** (Stevens Ave.) in May to see warblers, thrushes, and other migratory birds that gather in the ponds and meadows. During peak periods it's possible to see as many as 20 warbler species in a morning, including the Cape May, bay breasted, mourning, and Tennessee. Naturalists from Maine Audubon often are onsite helping to identify birds. For more info, check the events calendar at www.mainebirding.net.

SCARBOROUGH

Scarborough Beach Park (Black Point Rd./ Rte. 207, 207/883-2416, www.scarboroughbeachstatepark.com, $6.50 nonresident adults, $4.50 Maine resident adults, $2 children), a long stretch of sand, is the best beach for big waves. Between the parking area and the lovely stretch of beach you'll pass Massacre Pond, named for a 1703 skirmish between resident Native Americans and wannabe residents (score: Indians 19, wannabes 0). The park is open all year for swimming, surfing (permit

WINSLOW HOMER

© HILARY NANGLE

Plan in advance to tour the masterfully restored Prouts Neck studio of painter Winslow Homer.

Discovering Maine in his early 40s, Winslow Homer (1836-1910) was smitten—enough to spend the last 27 years of his life in Prouts Neck, a thumb of land edged with beaches and tipped with granite reaching into the Atlantic in Scarborough, just south of Portland. Homer painted some of his greatest works—masterpieces such as *Weatherbeaten, The Fog Warning,* and *The Gulf Stream*—at this oceanfront studio, taking inspiration from the crashing surf, craggy shores, stormy seas, and dense fog. Standing in the studio puts you right at the scene, and the docent-led tours will explain the artist's importance in American art.

Originally the carriage house for Homer's *The Ark,* the adjacent house owned by Homer's brother Charles, the studio was moved 100 feet and converted to living quarters in 1883 by Port-

land architect John Calvin Stevens, one of the founders of the Shingle style. The piazza, pergola, and later the painting room were added.

The simplicity of the studio, with its beadboard wall and ceiling, tongue-and-groove floor, and brick fireplace, is pure Maine cottage. Some original furnishings and artifacts add context to understanding Homer. These include the *Snakes! Snakes! Mice!* sign he painted to scare off ladies who might be inclined to visit; the window in which he etched his name; the writings on the wall, such as *Oh what a friend chance can be when it chooses;* and a book of family photographs. Copies of his artwork, displays, and a slide show of images are exhibited in the painting room, or "the factory," as he called it. Especially intriguing are the Civil War sketches he made for *Harper's Weekly* while embedded with the Army of the Potomac.

The views from the second-floor piazza are the same as when Homer lived here. Gazing at the open Atlantic, listening to waves crash, gulls cry, and the wind rustling the trees, and maybe wrapped in the damp hush of fog, is perhaps the best place to begin to truly understand Homer's inspiration. After absorbing the view and walking to the oceanfront, you'll see the Homer works at the museum with a far deeper understanding of what made this genius tick.

Homer's ties with the Portland Museum of Art date back to his 1893 exhibition, which included *Signal of Distress.* On the centennial of Homer's death, the museum opened its Charles Shipman Payson wing, honoring the man who funded it and donated 17 paintings by the artist. The museum acquired Homer's studio, a National Historic Landmark, in 2006, opening it to the public after a six-year project to restore it to its 1910 appearance. The 2.5-hour tours are limited to 10 participants and cost $55 for the public, $30 for museum members. They depart the museum three times daily, Tuesday through Sunday, from early May through mid-June and late September to early December. Reservations are required.

required), beachcombing, and ice skating, but on weekends in summer the parking lot fills early.

At 3,100 acres, **Scarborough Marsh** (Pine Point Rd./Rte. 9, 207/883-5100, www.maine-audubon.org, 9:30am-5:30pm daily mid-June-early Sept., 9:30am-5:30pm Sat.-Sun. late May and Sept.), Maine's largest salt marsh, is prime territory for bird-watching and canoeing. Rent a canoe ($16 for 1 hour, $23 for 1.5 hours, $30 for 2 hours) at the small nature center operated by Maine Audubon and explore on your own. Or join one of the 90-minute guided tours (call for the schedule, $12). Other special programs, some geared primarily for children, include wildflower walks, art classes, and dawn bird-watching trips; all require reservations and very reasonable fees. Also here is a walking-tour trail of less than one mile. Pick up a map at the center.

Overlooking the marsh is 52-acre **Scarborough River Wildlife Sanctuary** (Pine Point Rd./Rte. 9), with 1.5 miles of walking trails that loop to the Scarborough River and past two ponds.

FALMOUTH

A 65-acre wildlife sanctuary and environmental center on the banks of the Presumpscot River, **Gilsland Farm** (20 Gilsland Farm Rd., 207/781-2330, www.maineaudubon.org, dawn-dusk daily) is state headquarters for Maine Audubon. More than two miles of easy, well-marked trails wind through the grounds, taking in salt marshes, rolling meadows, woodlands, and views of the estuary. Observation blinds allow inconspicuous spying during bird-migration season. In the education center (9am-5pm Mon.-Sat., noon-4pm Sun.) are hands-on exhibits, a nature store, and classrooms and offices. Fees are charged for special events, but otherwise it's all free. The visitors center is 0.25 mile off Route 1.

Once the summer compound of the prominent Baxter family, Falmouth's 100-acre **Mackworth Island** (sunrise-sunset daily year-round), reached via a causeway, is now the site of the Governor Baxter School for the Deaf. Limited parking is just beyond the security booth on the island. On the 1.5-mile vehicle-free perimeter path, which has great Portland Harbor views, you'll meet bikers, hikers, and dog walkers. Just off the trail on the north side of the island is the late governor Percival Baxter's stone-circled pet cemetery, maintained by the state at the behest of Baxter, who donated this island as well as Baxter State Park to the people of Maine. From downtown Portland, take Route 1 across the Presumpscot River to Falmouth Foreside. Andrews Avenue (third street on the right) leads to the island.

Walking Tours
PORTLAND FREEDOM TRAIL

Pick up a copy of this free map and brochure (also available online) detailing a self-guided walking tour of 16 marked sights related to Portland's role in Maine's Underground Railroad (www.portlandfreedomtrail.org). Among the highlights are the Abyssinian Meeting House, the third-oldest African American meetinghouse still standing in the United States (currently undergoing restoration); the First Parish Unitarian Universalist Church, where abolitionist William Lloyd Garrison spoke in 1832; and Mariners' Church, location of an antislavery bookstore and print shop that printed the first Afrocentric history of the world.

PORTLAND WOMEN'S HISTORY TRAIL

Another self-guided walking tour, this one details four loops—Congress Street, Munjoy Hill, State Street, and the West End—with about 20 stops on each. Among the sites: a long-gone chewing-gum factory where teenage girls worked 10-hour shifts. The trail guide is available online (www.usm.maine.edu/~history/

newtrail.html) or for $8.50 in selected bookstores and at the Maine History Gallery gift shop (489 Congress St., 207/879-0427).

GREATER PORTLAND LANDMARKS

Greater Portland Landmarks (207/774-5561, www.portlandlandmarks.org) sponsors neighborhood walking tours as well as an annual **summer tour program** that features four or five walking trips and excursions to offshore islands, historic churches, revamped buildings, and gardens. Many of the destinations are private or otherwise inaccessible, so these are special opportunities. Registration is limited, and there's only one trip to each site. Tours run mid-July–mid-October, primarily on weekends.

MAINE FOODIE TOURS

Just as the name promises, Maine Foodie Tours (10 Moulton St., 207/233-7485, www.mainefoodietours.com) delivers a taste of Maine. The Old Port Culinary Walking Tour ($39) visits vendors selling everything from cheese to lobster to chocolate; Culinary Delights Trolley Tour ($40) includes both onboard and in-shop tastings. Other options include a chocolate tour, bike and brews tour, and progressive island cruise.

Land-and-Sea Tours

Various commercial operators offer area land-and-sea tours, but frankly, none is first-rate. Guides on each often present incorrect information. Still, such tours are a good way to get the city's general layout.

The best of the lot is the 1.5-hour narrated sightseeing tour of Portland in a trolley-bus by **Portland Discovery Land and Sea Tours** (3 Moulton St., Old Port, 207/774-0808, www.portlanddiscovery.com, $21 adults, $15 children). You can combine this tour with a 90-minute Lighthouse Lovers cruise on Casco Bay. The combined price is $39 adults, $27 children.

◖ CASCO BAY TOUR

Casco Bay Lines (Commercial St. and Franklin St., Old Port, 207/774-7871, www.cascobaylines.com), the nation's oldest continuously operating ferry system (since the 1920s), is the lifeline between Portland and six inhabited Casco Bay islands. What better way to sample the islands than to take the three-hour ride along with mail, groceries, and island residents? The Casco Bay Lines mail boat stops—briefly—at **Long Island, Chebeague, Cliff,** and **Little Diamond** and **Great Diamond Islands.** Departures are 10am and 2:15pm daily mid-June–Labor Day, 10am and 2:45pm in other months. Fares are $15.50 adults, $14.50 seniors, and $7.75 ages 5-9. The longest cruise on the Casco Bay Lines schedule is the nearly six-hour narrated summertime trip (late June–early Sept., $25 adults, $22 seniors, $12 ages 5-9) with a two-hour stopover on **Bailey Island,** departing from Portland at 10am daily. Dogs ($3.75) on leashes and bicycles ($7) need separate tickets.

Bicycling

The **Bicycle Coalition of Maine** (207/623-4511, www.bikemaine.org) has an excellent website with info on trails, events, organized rides, bike shops, and more. Another good resource is **Casco Bay Bicycle Club** (www.cascobaybicycleclub.org), a recreational cycling club with rides several times weekly. Check the website for details.

For rentals (hybrids $25 per day) and repairs, visit **Cycle Mania** (59 Federal St., 207/774-2933, www.cyclemania1.com).

The best locales for island bicycling—fun for families and beginners but not especially challenging for diehards—are Peaks and Great Chebeague Islands, but do remember to follow the rules of the road.

Golf

Public courses are plentiful in Greater

© HILARY NANGLE

Hop on one of the Casco Bay ferries for an island excursion.

Portland, but you'll need an "in" to play the private ones. Free advice on helping you choose a course is offered by **Golf Maine** (www.info@golfme.com).

Consider just Greater Portland's 18-hole courses. **Sable Oaks Golf Club** (505 Country Club Dr., South Portland, 207/775-6257, www.sableoaks.com) is considered one of the toughest and best of Maine's public courses. Since 1998, **Nonesuch River Golf Club** (304 Gorham Rd./Rte. 114, Scarborough, 207/883-0007 or 888/256-2717, www.nonesuchgolf.com) has been drawing raves for the challenges of its par-70 championship course and praise from environmentalists for preserving wildlife habitat; there's also a full-size practice range and green. The City of Portland's **Riverside Municipal Golf Course** (1158 Riverside St., 207/797-3524) has an 18-hole par-72 course (Riverside North) and a nine-hole par-35 course (Riverside South). Opt for the 18-hole course.

Sea Kayaking

With all the islands scattered through Casco Bay, Greater Portland is a sea-kayaking hotbed. The best place to start is out on Peaks Island, 15 minutes offshore via Casco Bay Lines ferry. **Maine Island Kayak Company** (MIKCO, 70 Luther St., Peaks Island, 207/766-2373 or 800/796-2373, www.maineislandkayak.com) organizes half-day, all-day, and multiday local kayaking trips as well as national and international adventures. An introductory half-day tour in Casco Bay is $70 pp; a full day is $110 pp and includes lunch. Reservations are essential. MIKCO also does private lessons and group courses and clinics (some require previous experience). MIKCO's owner, Tom Bergh, has a flawless reputation for safety and skill.

◖ Lobstering Cruise

Learn all kinds of lobster lore and maybe even catch your own dinner with **Lucky Catch Lobster Tours** (170 Commercial St.,

207/233-2026 or 888/624-6321, www.lucky-catch.com, $25 adults, $22 seniors, $20 ages 13-18, $15 ages 2-12). Captain Tom Martin offers four different 80-90-minute cruises on his 37-foot lobster boat. On each cruise (except late Saturday and all day Sunday, when state law prohibits it), usually 10 traps are hauled and the process and gear are explained. You can even help if you want. Any lobsters caught are available for purchase after the cruise for wholesale boat price (and you can have them cooked nearby for a reasonable rate). Wouldn't that make a nice story to tell the folks back home?

Boat Excursions

Down on the Old Port wharves are several excursion-boat businesses. Each has carved out a niche, so choose according to your interest and your schedule. Dress warmly and wear rubber-soled shoes. Remember that all cruises are weather-dependent.

Portland Discover-Land & Sea Tours (Long Wharf, 207/774-0808, www.portland-discovery.com) offers a Lighthouse Lovers Cruise and a Sunset Lighthouse Cruise ($21 adults, $15 children).

Cruise up to 20 miles offshore seeking whales with **Odyssey Whale Watch** (Long Wharf, 170 Commercial St., 207/775-0727, www.odysseywhalewatch.com, $48 adults, $38 under age 12). Four-five-hour whale watches aboard the *Odyssey* depart daily June-early September as well as on spring and fall weekends. (Go easy on breakfast that day, and take preventive measures if you're motion sensitive.)

Sail quietly across the waters of Casco Bay aboard a windjammer with **Portland Schooner Company** (Maine State Pier, 56 Commercial St., 207/766-2500, www.portlandschooner.com, late May-Oct., $39 adults, $15 age 12 and under). Four to six two-hour sails are offered daily on two schooners, the 72-foot *Bagheera*

sightseeing on a Portland boat tour

COURTESY OF PORTLAND CONVENTION & VISITORS BUREAU

and the 88-foot *Wendameen,* both historical vessels designed by John G. Alden and built in East Boothbay. Overnight windjammer trips also are available for $250 pp, including dinner and breakfast.

Spectator Sports

A pseudo-fierce mascot named Slugger stirs up the crowds at baseball games played by the **Portland Sea Dogs** (Hadlock Field, 271 Park Ave., 207/879-9500 or 800/936-3647, www.portlandseadogs.com, less than $10), a AA Boston Red Sox farm team. The season schedule (early Apr.-Aug.) is available after January 1.

For ice hockey action, the AHL affiliate **Portland Pirates** (207/775-3458, www.portlandpirates.com, $16-20) plays winter and spring home games at the Cumberland County Civic Center (1 Civic Center Sq.).

The newest entry among Portland's professional teams is the **Red Claws** (207/210-6655, www.maineredclaws.com, $10-30), an NBA development team for the Boston Celtics. Home court is the Portland Expo (239 Park Ave.).

ACCOMMODATIONS
Downtown Portland

Portland's peninsula doesn't have an overwhelming amount of sleeping space, but it does have good variety in all price ranges. Rates reflect peak season.

INNS AND BED-AND-BREAKFASTS

All of these are in older buildings without elevators; stairs may be steep.

Railroad tycoon John Deering built **The Inn at St. John** (939 Congress St., 207/773-6481 or 800/636-9127, www.innatstjohn.com, $85-250) in 1897. The comfortable (if somewhat tired) moderately priced 37-room hostelry welcomes children and pets and even has bicycle storage. Cable TV, air-conditioning, free local calls, free parking, free airport pickup, and a meager continental breakfast are provided. Most guest rooms have private baths (some are detached); some have fridges and microwaves. The downside is the lackluster neighborhood—in the evening you'll want to drive or take a taxi when going out. It's about a 35-minute walk to the Old Port or an $8 taxi fare.

Staying at ◖ **The Pomegranate Inn** (49 Neal St. at Carroll St., 207/772-1006 or 800/356-0408, www.pomegranateinn.com, $190-300) is an adventure in itself, with faux paintings, classical statuary, contemporary art, antiques, and whimsical touches everywhere—you'll either love it or find it a bit much. The elegant 1884 Italianate mansion has seven guest rooms and a suite, all with air-conditioning, TV, and Wi-Fi, some with fireplaces.

Take a carefully renovated 1830s town house, add contemporary amenities and a service-oriented innkeeper, and the result is the **Morrill Mansion Bed and Breakfast** (249 Vaughan St., 207/774-6900 or 888/566-7745, www.morrillmansion.com, $149-239), on the West End. Six guest rooms and one suite are spread out on the second and third floors. No frilly Victorian accents here—the decor is understated yet tasteful, taking advantage of hardwood floors and high ceilings. You'll find free Wi-Fi and local calls and a TV with a DVD player in each room. A continental breakfast is included; off-street parking is free. It's near the hospital, so you might hear a siren or two.

In the same neighborhood is **The Chadwick Bed & Breakfast** (140 Chadwick St., 800/774-2137, www.thechadwick.com, $200-225). All rooms have flat-screen TVs with DVD players, iPod docking stations, and Wi-Fi, and a DVD library is available. Here's a nice service: If you need to depart before the full breakfast is served, a bagged breakfast is provided.

Innkeeper Buddy Marcum welcomes guests warmly and treats them like royalty with plush linens and memorable breakfasts at **The Carleton Inn** (46 Carlton St., 207/775-1910 or 800/639-1779, www.innoncarleton.com, $185-200), a masterfully updated and decorated 1869 Victorian with a convenient location in the city's West End. Although all guest rooms have private baths, two are detached.

Former travel writer Dale Northrup put his experience to work in opening the **Percy Inn** (15 Pine St., 207/871-7638 or 888/417-3729, www.percyinn.com, $149-209), conveniently located just off Longfellow Square. The air-conditioned guest rooms are furnished with phones, CD players, TV/VCRs, wet bars, and refrigerators. There's even a 24-hour pantry. It's best suited for independent-minded travelers who don't desire much contact with the host or other guests, as public rooms are few and the innkeeper, although always accessible, is rarely on-site. Breakfast is a continental buffet. Off-street parking is free. If you're noise sensitive, avoid accommodations that open directly into the pantry, kitchen, or breakfast room.

Built in 1835, **The Inn at Park Spring** (135 Spring St., 207/774-1059 or 800/427-8511, www.innatparkspring.com, $149-205) is one of Portland's longest-running bed-and-breakfasts. The location is excellent, just steps from most Arts District attractions. Six somewhat quirky guest rooms are spread out on three floors. All have air-conditioning and phones, and some have Internet access; one has a private patio and entrance. There's a guest fridge on each floor. Rates include a full breakfast served around a common table.

The handsome Georgian-style **West End Inn** (146 Pine St. at Neal St., 800/338-1377, www.westendbb.com, $160-195), built in 1877, has six guest rooms on three floors; one with de-tached bath, one with private deck. The decor blends traditional furnishings with contemporary accents. A full breakfast and afternoon refreshments are served.

FULL-SERVICE HOTELS

The ◖ **Portland Harbor Hotel** (468 Fore St., 207/775-9090 or 888/798-9090, www.portlandharborhotel.com, from $299), an upscale boutique hotel in the Old Port, is built around a garden courtyard. Rooms are plush, with chic linens, duvets, down pillows on the beds, Wi-Fi, and digital cable TV; marble and granite bathrooms have separate soaking tubs and showers. Complimentary bike rentals are available, and the hotel offers a free local car service. There's a cozy lounge, and the excellent restaurant has 24-hour room service. Also on the premises are a fitness room and spa services. The best splurge is the suites, added in 2009. Ice Bar, which features bars made of ice, is held the last weekend of January in the hotel's courtyard and draws a crowd.

You might have trouble finding the **Portland Regency** (20 Milk St., 207/774-4200 or 800/727-3436, www.theregency.com, from $290): This hotel, registered with the National Trust for Historic Preservation as a historic property, is secreted in a renovated armory in the heart of the Old Port. The nicest rooms are the renovated ones, especially those on the fourth floor with decks. Perks include Wi-Fi and free shuttles to all major Portland transportation facilities. Be forewarned: Room configurations vary widely—some provide little natural window light or are strangely shaped. All have LCD TVs, minibars, and air-conditioning. A restaurant, spa, and fitness center are on-site.

Yes, it's a chain, and yes, it's downright ugly, but the **Holiday Inn by the Bay** (88 Spring St., 207/775-2311 or 800/345-5050, www.innbythebay.com, from $175) provides a lot of bang for the buck. It's conveniently situated between the waterfront and the Arts District. Rooms on upper floors have views either over Back Cove or Portland Harbor; Wi-Fi and parking are free, as is a local shuttle service. It also has

© HILARY NANGLE

GREATER PORTLAND

The Inn by the Sea, in Cape Elizabeth, edges Crescent Beach and the Atlantic.

an indoor pool, a sauna, a fitness room, on-site laundry facilities, a restaurant, and a lounge.

The Burbs

South of Portland are two upscale beachfront inns. Especially splurge-worthy and well suited for families is the oceanfront **C Inn by the Sea** (40 Bowery Beach Rd./Rte. 77, Cape Elizabeth, 207/799-3134 or 800/888-4287, www.innbythesea.com, from around $490), just seven miles south of downtown Portland. Guests stay in handsome rooms, suites, and cottages, most with kitchens or expanded wet bars, comfy living rooms, and big views. This is perhaps Southern Maine's most contemporary luxury property, with a cozy lounge, a full-service spa, and a small cardio room. Big windows frame ocean views at **Sea Glass** (207/299-3134, entrées $23-34), where chef Mitchell Kaldrovich favors Maine ingredients in his creative breakfasts, lunches, and dinners. Other facilities include an outdoor pool, a *boules* court, wildlife

habitats, and a private boardwalk winding through a salt marsh to the southern end of Crescent Beach State Park. By reservation, dogs are honored guests; they're welcomed with bowls and bed, receive turn-down treats, and have their own room service and spa menus.

The **Black Point Inn Resort** (510 Black Point Rd., Prouts Neck, Scarborough, 207/883-2500 or 800/258-0003, www.blackpointinn.com, from $260 pp, includes breakfast, afternoon tea, and dinner) is a classic, unpretentious seaside hotel with a genteel vibe. The historic shingle-style hotel opened in 1878 at the tip of Prouts Neck, overlooking Casco Bay from one side and down to Old Orchard from the other. Now owned by a local partnership, the inn has returned to its roots, catering to wealthy rusticators. The Point Restaurant is open to nonguests by reservation (6pm-8:30pm daily, $28-38), and the less-fussy Chart Room (11:30am-9pm daily, $10-18) serves lighter fare—but first, enjoy cocktails on the porch

© HILARY NANGLE

The Black Point Inn Resort is located on Prouts Neck, near the studio of painter Winslow Homer.

at sunset, with views over beach and water to distant Mt. Washington. Guests have access to a private, oceanfront 18-hole golf course and tennis courts, the Cliff Walk around the point (passing American master Winslow Homer's studio, recently opened to the public by reserved guided tour departing from the Portland Museum of Art), and a lovely trail-laced woodland sanctuary that has ties to Homer's family. A hefty 18 percent service charge is added to daily rates.

Only a narrow byway separates **The Breakers Inn** (2 Bay View Ave., Higgins Beach, Scarborough, 207/883-4820, www.thebreakersinn.com, $185 daily, $1,000 weekly) from the sands of Higgins Beach. This is an old-timey bed-and-breakfast in a turreted, porch-wrapped three-story Victorian. It was built in 1900, converted to an inn in the 1930s, and has been operated by the Laughton family since 1956. Every room in the main inn has an ocean

view, including two in the basement. Interior stairways are steep and narrow. Fancy or frilly, this isn't; you're paying for location, not amenities or decor. Picnic lunches are available. No credit cards.

FOOD

Named "America's Foodiest Small Town" by *Bon Appétit* magazine in 2009, downtown Portland alone has more than 100 restaurants, so it's impossible to list even all the great ones—and there are many. The city's proximity to fresh foods from both farms and the sea makes it popular with chefs, and its growing immigrant population means a good choice of ethnic dining too. Here is a choice selection, by neighborhood, with open days and hours provided for peak season. Some restaurants don't list a closing time; that's because they shut the doors when the crowd thins, so to be safe, call ahead if you're heading out much after 8pm.

Do make reservations whenever possible and as far in advance as you can, especially in July-August. If you're especially into the food scene, check www.portlandfoodmap.com for a breakdown by cuisine of Portland restaurants with links to recent reviews.

In addition to the many restaurant options listed here, check the "Community News" listings in each Wednesday's *Portland Press Herald.* Under "Potluck," you'll find listings of **public meals**, usually benefiting nonprofit organizations. Prices are always quite low (under $10 for adults, $2-4 for children), mealtimes quite early (5 or 6pm), and the flavor quite local.

When you need a java fix, **Coffee by Design** (620 Congress St.; 67 India St.; 43 Washington Ave., 207/879-2233) is the local choice, not only for its fine brews but also for its support of local artists and community causes.

The Portland Farmers Market sets up on Wednesday on Monument Square and on Saturday in Deering Oaks Park.

Days and hours of operation listed below reflect peak season and are subject to change.

The Old Port and the Waterfront
LOCAL FLAVORS

All of these venues are west of the Franklin Street Arterial between Congress and Commercial Streets.

Best known for the earliest and most filling breakfast, **Becky's Diner** (390 Commercial St., 207/773-7070, www.beckysdiner.com, 4am-9pm daily) has more than a dozen omelet choices, just for a start. It also serves lunch and dinner, all at downright cheap prices.

Enjoy pizza with a view at **Flatbread Company** (72 Commercial St., 207/772-8777, www.flatbreadcompany.com, 11:30am-10pm daily), part of a small New England chain. The all-natural pizza is baked in a primitive wood-fired clay oven and served in a dining room with a wall of windows overlooking the ferry

terminal and Portland Harbor. Vegan options are available.

For gourmet goodies, don't miss **Browne Trading Market** (Merrill's Wharf, 262 Commercial St., 207/775-7560). Owner Rod Mitchell became the Caviar King of Portland by wholesaling Caspian caviar, and now he's letting the rest of us in on it. Fresh fish and shellfish fill the cases next to the caviar and cheeses. The mezzanine is literally wall-to-wall wine, specializing in French.

When you're craving carbs, want pastries for breakfast, or need to boost your energy with a sweet, follow your nose to **Standard Baking Company** (75 Commercial St., 207/773-2112), deservedly famous for its handcrafted breads and pastries.

CASUAL DINING
Walter's (2 Portland Sq., 207/871-9258, www.waltersportland.com, 11:30am-9pm Mon.-Fri., 5pm-9pm Sat., $23-28) has been serving creative fusion fare since the 1990s (although in a chic new location as of late 2009). Despite the longevity, it's never tiresome and retains well-earned status as a favored go-to among the city's foodie set.

Chef-entrepreneur Harding Lee Smith's **The Grill Room** (84 Exchange St., 207/774-2333, www.thefrontroomrestaurant.com, 11:30am-2:30pm Mon.-Sat. and from 5-daily, $18-39) turns out excellent wood-grilled meats and seafood.

Small plates and big flavors come from the open kitchen of **The Salt Exchange** (245 Commercial St., 207/347-5687, www.thesaltexchange.net, 11:30am-3pm Mon.-Sat. and 5:30pm-9pm Mon.-Thurs., to 10pm Fri.-Sat.), a contemporary restaurant and lounge decorated with local artwork that changes quarterly. You'll probably want to order at least three plates ($9-26 each) to make a meal. The restaurant also has Maine's largest bourbon selection.

GREATER PORTLAND

SEAFOOD

Ask around and everyone will tell you the best seafood in town is at **Street and Company** (33 Wharf St., 207/775-0887, www.streetandcompany.net, opens 5:30pm daily, $22-32). Fresh, beautifully prepared fish is what you get, often with a Mediterranean flair. Tables are tight, and it's often noisy in the informal brick-walled rooms.

For a broader seafood menu and more land-lubber options, consider **Old Port Sea Grille and Raw Bar** (93 Commercial St., 207/879-6100, www.theoldportseagrill.com, from 11:30am daily, from $23), a sleek, modern spot near the waterfront with a fabulous raw bar and a 500-gallon aquarium inside.

For lobster in the rough, head to **Portland Lobster Company** (180 Commercial St., 207/775-2112, www.portlandlobstercompany.com, 11am-10pm daily). There's a small inside seating area, but it's much more pleasant to sit out on the wharf and watch the excursion boats come and go. Expect to pay in the low $20 range for a one-pound lobster with fries and slaw. Other choices ($8-23) and a kids menu are available.

ETHNIC FARE

Sushi approaches an art form at **Miyake** (468 Fore St., 207/871-9170, www.miyakerestaurants.com, 11:30am-2:30pm and 5:30pm-10pm Mon.-Sat., 1pm-1:45pm and 5pm-9pm Sun., from $23). Trained in both French and classical Japanese techniques, chef Masa Miyake has developed a following far beyond Maine for his innovative sushi, crafted from primarily local ingredients, including vegetables, fowl, and pork raised on his farm.

Be forewarned: Your first foray into **❰ Bresca** (111 Middle St., 207/772-1004, www.restaurantbresca.com, lunch from 11:30am Wed.-Sat., dinner from 5:30pm Fri.-Sat., $28) won't be your last. Chef Krista Kerns Desjarlais delivers big flavor in this tiny Mediterranean-flavored space next to Portland's police station. She shops each morning, buying just enough for that night's meal (yes, items do sell out). You'll need a reservation to land one of the 20 seats. Service is personal, the meal is leisurely, and the food is divine. Save room for dessert: Krista initially made her name as a pastry chef.

Top-notch for northern Italian is **Vignola Cinque Terre Ristorante** (36 Wharf St., 207/347-6154, www.cinqueterremaine.com, from 5pm daily, lunch from 11:30am Fri.-Sat., brunch from 10am Sun., $12-34). Chef Lee Skawinski is committed to sustainable farming, and much of the seasonal and organic produce used comes from the restaurant owners' Laughing Stock Farm and other Maine farms. Choose from half- or full-size portions.

The Corner Room Kitchen and Bar (110 Exchange St., 207/879-4747, www.thefrontroomrestaurant.com, from 11:30am Mon.-Sat., 10am-3 p.m. and 4pm-9pm Sun., $15-29), another of popular local chef Harding Lee Smith's restaurants, takes its cue from rustic Italian fare, with hearty and delicious pizzas, pastas, and paninis.

Pasta doesn't get much more authentic than that served at **Paciarino** (468 Fore St., 207/774-3500, www.paciarino.com, 11:30am-2:30pm and 6pm-9pm daily, $13-20). Owners Fabiana De Savino and Enrico Barbiero moved here from Milan in 2008, and they make their pastas and sauces fresh daily using recipes from De Savino's *nonna*.

You might think you've landed in Paris at Jean Claude Vassalle's **Merry Table Creperie** (43 Wharf St., 207/899-4494, 11:30am-2:30pm and 5pm-9pm Mon.-Sat., 11am-3pm Sun.), a charming French country bistro specializing in savory and sweet crepes ($9-13).

Irish fare with a Maine accent fills the menu at **Ri-Ra** (72 Commercial St., 207/761-4446, www.rira.com/portland, 11:30am-10pm daily). Entrées in the glass-walled second-floor dining room, overlooking the Casco Bay Lines ferry terminal, are $10-22. The ground-floor pub, elegantly woody with an enormous bar, is inevitably stuffed to the gills on weekends—a great spot for such traditional fare as corned beef and cabbage as long as you can stand the din. They don't take reservations, so be prepared to wait, especially on weekends.

For New World flavors in an Old World setting, dine at **Sonny's** (83 Exchange St., 207/772-7774, www.sonnysportland.com, lunch 11:30am-2 and from 5pm daily, $7-22), in a former bank, serving Southwestern and South American foods such as a tri-pork Cuban sandwich or banana-leaf-baked whitefish.

DESTINATION DINING

Plan well in advance to land a reservation at **Fore Street** (288 Fore St., 207/775-2717, www.forestreet.biz, 5:30pm-10pm Sun.-Thurs., 5:30pm-10:30pm Fri.-Sat., entrées from $20). Chef Sam Hayward, renowned for his passionate and creative use of Maine-sourced ingredients, won the James Beard Award for Best Chef in the Northeast in 2004 and has been featured in most of the foodie publications. Hayward excels at elevating simple foods to into rave-worthy dishes. The renovated former warehouse has copper-topped tables, an open kitchen, and industrial decor chic—quiet it's not. Make reservations well in advance, or show up early to try to land one of the handful of unreserved tables.

Arts District

These restaurants are clustered around Danforth Street and along and around Congress Street.

LOCAL FLAVORS

Can't make up your mind? Peruse the reasonably priced fare available at **Public Market House** (28 Monument Sq., 207/228-2056, www.publicmarkethouse.com, 8am-7pm Mon.-Sat., 10am-5pm Sun.), with vendors selling meats, cheeses, breads, sandwiches, pizzas, burritos, coffees, and soups.

Be sure to have a reservation if you're going before the theater to **BiBo's Madd Apple Café** (23 Forest Ave., 207/774-9698, www.bibosportland.com, 11:30am-2pm Wed.-Fri. and from 5:30pm Wed.-Sat., 10am-2pm Sun., from $17)—it's right next to the Portland Performing Arts Center. On the other hand, it's popular anytime thanks to chef Bill Boutwell ("BiBo"). There's no way of predicting what will be on the bistro-fusion menu.

Well off most visitors' radar screens is **Artemisia Café** (61 Pleasant St., 207/761-0135, 11am-2pm Mon.-Fri., 9am-2pm Sat.-Sun.), a cheery neighborhood café with a creative menu drawing on international influences.

Nosh (551 Congress St., 207/553-2227, www.noshkitchenbar.com, 11:30am-1am Mon.-Sat., 4pm-1am Sun.) updates the concept of New York-style deli fare with a fresh-and-local twist. The setting is sleek, with a granite bar on one side, copper-topped tables on the other, and comfy loungelike seating at the entry. Nosh serves inspired salads, sandwiches, and burgers by day ($9-20). At night, the menu expands to include charcuterie and artisanal cheese plates and other offerings. Be sure to order the fries, offered in flavors including bacon-dusted and salt-and-vinegar, and accompanied by a choice from a tempting array of mayos, cheese sauces, and even *sriracha* sauce, a type of hot sauce.

ETHNIC AND VEGETARIAN FARE

Slip into sleek **Emilitsa** (547 Congress St., 207/221-0245, www.emilitsa.com, from 5pm Tues.-Sat., $18-35) for finely crafted authentic Greek food paired with Greek wines.

Duck into chef-owner Asmeret Teklu's **Asmara** (51 Oak St., 207/253-5122, 11:30am-2pm and 5pm-9pm Tues.-Fri., 5pm-9pm Sat., entrées $9-14) to be transported to eastern

Africa. Traditional Eritrean and Ethiopian dishes, a mix of mild to spicy curried stews, and vegetarian plates are served on *injera,* spongy flat bread made from teff flour that doubles as an eating utensil (silverware is available, if you ask). Entrées are generous and come with a salad and choice of vegetable. Service is leisurely; this is a one-woman show.

Masa Miyake's **Pai Men Miyake** (188 State St., 207/541-9204, www.miyakerestaurants. com, noon-midnight Mon.-Sat., to 10pm Sun., $7-16) is a traditional Japanese noodle bar serving miso and ramen soup along with amazing pork gyoza and pork buns. It's open for lunch and dinner, but call for details.

Ever-popular **Local 188** (685 Congress St., 207/761-7909, www.local188.com, from 5:30pm daily and 9am-2pm Sat.-Sun.) serves fabulous Mediterranean-inspired food with a tapas-heavy menu. It doubles as an art gallery with rotating exhibits. Most tapas selections are less than $10; heartier choices and entrées begin at $18. There is free parking behind the building.

Authentic Thai—not the Americanized version but the kind of food you might purchase from a street vendor in Bangkok—is served in a very non-Thai, cool-yet-sophisticated space at **Boda** (671 Congress St., 207/347-7557, www.bodamaine.com, 5pm-1am Tues.-Sun.). Make a meal out of small plates, or opt for an entrée ($12-19); vegetarian and gluten-free dishes are available.

Hearty, homestyle German fare is the draw at **Schulte & Herr** (349 Cumberland Ave., 207/773-1997, 11:30am-2pm Wed.-Fri., 8am-2:30pm Sun., and 5pm-9pm Wed.-Sat., $15-18).

Vegan and vegetarian cuisine comes with an Asian accent at **Green Elephant** (608 Congress St., 207/347-3111, www.greenelephantmaine.com, 11:30am-2:30pm Tues.-Sat. and from 5pm daily, $9-14). There's not one shred of meat on the creative menu, but you won't miss it.

Just outside the Arts District, **El Rayo Taqueria** (101 York St., 207/780-8226, www. elrayotaqueria.com, 11am-9pm daily), in a former gas station, delivers Cal-Mex flavors, with almost everything costing less (often far less) than $10. The prices go up a bit in the fancier and adjacent **Cantina El Rayo** (www.elrayocantina.com, from 5pm daily, $12-17).

Little Lad's (482 Congress St., 207/871-1636, www.littlelads.com, 11am-6pm Sun.-Fri.) is a no-frills vegan café, where the $4.99 lunch buffet, served 11am-3pm Mon.-Fri., might include chick-in cacciatore or bean stroganoff. Also available are sandwiches and sweets. Don't miss the herbal popcorn.

CASUAL DINING

Fun, whimsical, and artsy describes most restaurants in the Arts District, but not **Five Fifty-Five** (555 Congress St., 207/761-0555, www.fivefifty-five.com, from 5pm daily and 9:30am-2pm Sun., $10-32), where chef Steve Corry was named by *Food & Wine* magazine as one of the top 10 Best New Chefs in the country. Fresh, local, and seasonal are blended in creative ways on his ever-changing menu, which is divided into small plates, green plates, savory plates, cheese plates, and sweet plates. A five-course tasting menu is around $60. If you can't afford to splurge in the main restaurant, Corry serves lighter fare in the lounge.

A longtimer in the Portland dining scene, **David's** (22 Monument Sq., 207/773-4340, www.davidsrestaurant.com, 11:30am-4pm Mon.-Fri. and from 5pm daily, $10-30) serves pizzas, pastas, and updated familiar fare. Never one to rest on his laurels, chef-owner David Turin opened **David's Opus 10,** an 18-seat fixed-price restaurant within this one in 2012, and has an equally popular restaurant in South Portland.

West End

Have breakfast or lunch or pick up prepared foods at **Aurora Provisions** (64 Pine St., 207/871-9060, www.auroraprovisions.com, 8am-6:30pm Mon.-Sat.), a combination market and café with irresistible goodies, most made on the premises.

Superb thin-crust pizzas made from all-natural ingredients in usual and unusual flavor combos emerge from the wood-fired oven at **Bonobo** (46 Pine St., 207/347-8267, www.bonobopizza.com, 11:30am-2:30pm Wed.-Fri., noon-4pm Sat., and from 4pm daily, $10-17).

Chef Abby Harmon's **Caiola's Restaurant** (58 Pine St., 207/772-1110, www.caiolas.com, from 5:30pm Mon.-Sat. and 9am-2pm Sun., entrées from $14) delivers comfort food with pizzazz in a cozy neighborhood bistro. This little gem is off most visitors' radar screens, but locals fill it nightly.

Bayside

Portlanders have long favored **Bintliff's American Café** (98 Portland St., 207/774-0005, www.bintliffscafe.com, 7am-2pm daily) for its breakfasts and brunches ($7-12); the menu is humongous. It doesn't take reservations on weekends, so expect to wait in line.

Breakfast is served all day at the **Miss Portland Diner** (140 Marginal Way, 207/210-6673, www.missportlanddiner.com, 7am-3pm Mon.-Tues., 7am-9pm Wed.-Sat.), a 1949 Worcester Diner (car no. 818) that was rescued, restored, and reopened in 2007. Snag a counter stool or a booth in the original dining car, not the addition, then treat yourself to breakfast for dinner. Sure, there are more traditional choices—soups, sandwiches, wraps, burgers, dogs, comfort foods, seafood plates and platters, or nightly dinner specials (most choices range $7-12)—but breakfast and diners go together like bacon and eggs. An added bonus: Parking is plentiful and free.

For an elegant meal in a true fine-dining setting, reserve a table at the **⟨ Back Bay Grill** (65 Portland St., near the main post office, 207/772-8833, www.backbaygrill.com, from 5:30pm Tues.-Sat.). The serene dining room is accented by a colorful mural; Arts and Crafts wall sconces cast a soft glow on the white linen-draped tables. The menu, which highlights fresh, seasonal ingredients, ranks among the best in the city, and the wine list is long and well chosen. Service is professional. Entrées are $19-36 and worth every penny.

East End

These dining spots are all east of the Franklin Street Arterial. Poke around this end of the city and you'll find quite a few ethnic hole-in-the-wall places on and around Washington Avenue. It's an ever-changing array, but if you're adventurous or budget confined, give one a try.

LOCAL FLAVORS

Chocoholics take note: When a craving strikes, head to **Dean's Sweets** (82 Middle St., 207/899-3664) for adult-flavored dark-chocolate truffles made without nuts.

Stop by **Maine Mead Works** (51 Washington Ave., 207/773-6323, www.mainemeadworks.com) for a tour and tasting of the company's fermented honey drinks; call for a current schedule.

If you're a tea fan, don't miss **Homegrown Herb & Tea** (195 Congress St., 207/774-3484, www.homegrownherbandtea.com), an ayurvedic shop that blends black, green, and herbal teas and serves light fare, including a delightful lavender shortbread.

The most incredible fries come from **⟨ Duckfat** (43 Middle St., 207/774-8080, www.duckfat.com, 11am-10pm daily $8-14), an ultracasual joint owned by James Beard Award-winning chef Rob Evans. Fries—fried in duck fat, of course—are served in a paper cone and accompanied by your choice of six sauces; the truffle ketchup is heavenly. Want to really harden those arteries? Order the *poutine,* Belgian fries topped with Maine cheese curd and homemade duck gravy. In addition, Duckfat serves paninis, soups, salads, and really good milk shakes; wine and beer are available.

Mainers love their Italian sandwiches, and **Amato's** (71 India St., 207/773-1682, www. amatos.com, 6:30am-11pm daily, entrées $10-16) is credited with creating this drool-worthy sub, usually made with ham, cheese, tomatoes, green peppers, black olives, and onions wrapped in a doughy roll and drizzled with olive oil. Also available are calzones, salads, and other Italian-inspired foods. Amato's has outlets throughout southern Maine; this one has outdoor patio seating.

Micucci's Grocery Store (45 India St., 207/775-1854) has been serving Portland's Italian community since 1949. It's a great stop for picnic fixings and a nice selection of inexpensive wines. It's also home to baker Stephen Lanzalotta's to-die-for breads, pastries, and pizzas.

Ever had a mashed potato pizza? You can get one as well as other intriguing choices at **Otto Pizza** (225 Congress St., 207/358-7551, www. ottoportland.com, from 11:30am daily).

Huge portions at rock-bottom prices make **Silly's** (40 Washington Ave., 207/772-0360, www.sillys.com, 11am-9pm Tues.-Fri., 9am-9pm Sat.-Sun.) an ever-popular choice among the young and budget-minded. The huge menu has lots of international flair along with veggie, vegan, gluten-free, and dairy-free options. A separate menu lists milk shakes in dozens of wacky flavors. The decor: vintage kitsch, 1950s Formica and chrome, and Elvis. The same menu is served at adjacent **Silly's with a Twist,** which also serves alcohol.

Traditional Salvadorian foods (think Mexican with attitude) have turned hole-in-the-wall **Tu Casa** (70 Washington Ave., 207/828-4971, www.tucasaportland.com, 11am-9pm Sun.-Fri.) into a must-visit for in-the-know foodies. It's also a budget find, with almost everything on the menu going for less than $10.

Just try *not* to walk out with something from **Two Fat Cats Bakery** (47 India St., 207/347-5144)—oh, the cookies! The breads! The pies!

CASUAL DINING

Blue Spoon (89 Congress St., 207/773-1116, www.bluespoonme.com, 11:30am-3pm Mon.-Fri., 5pm-9pm Mon.-Sat., 9am-3pm Sun., $11-25) was one of the first upscale eateries on Portland's gentrifying East End. Chef-owner David Iovino, who studied at the French Culinary Institute, has created a warm and welcoming neighborhood gem.

Big flavors come out of the small plates served at **Bar Lola** (100 Congress St., 207/775-5652, www.barlola.net, 5pm-10pm Wed.-Sat., $8-19), an intimate and cozy neighborhood bistro serving a tapas-oriented menu. You can opt for a four-course prix fixe ($36) or the Just Say "Feed Me" ($44).

Primo rustic Italian fare is the rule at **Ribollita** (41 Middle St., 207/774-2972, www. ribollitamaine.com, from 5pm Mon.-Sat., $13-20). You'll want reservations at this small, casual trattoria that's justly popular for delivering good food at fair prices; just be in the mood for a leisurely meal.

You never know what'll be on the menu (Indonesian chicken, North African stuffed peppers, maybe Caribbean shrimp cakes) at funky **Pepperclub** (78 Middle St., 207/772-0531, www.pepperclubrestaurant.com, from 5pm-9pm Sun.-Thurs., 5pm-10pm Fri.-Sat., $13-20), but take the risk. Vegetarian and vegan specials are always available, as are local and organic meats and seafood. If your kids are even vaguely adventuresome, they'll find food to like—and the prices are reasonable. In the morning, it morphs into **The Good Egg** (7-noon Tues.-Fri., 8am-1pm Sat.-Sun.), serving breakfast, including gluten-free foods.

The weekly changing menu at **Hugo's** (88 Middle St. at Franklin St., 207/774-8538, www.hugos.net, from 5:30pm Tues.-Sat.) showcases fresh and local fare. Expect to mix and match at least two or three of the choices ($13-17), which might include fried mussels, grilled swordfish belly, or skirt steak.

Love oysters? Don't miss **Eventide Oyster Co.** (86 Middle St., 207/774-8538, www.eventideoysterco.com, 11am-midnight daily), where the menu includes nearly two dozen oysters and other shellfish paired with sauces, as well as other seafood; mix and match from $3, with entrees around $25.

The Burbs

Gorgeous presentation, rare cheeses, a ripening room, and a knowledgeable staff all add up to making **The Cheese Iron** (200 Rte. 1, 207/883-4057, www.thecheeseiron.com) a major destination for cheeseheads. Add wine, sandwiches, and a handful of other gourmet goodies and you've got a first-class picnic or party.

Great sunset views over Portland's skyline, a casual atmosphere, and excellent fare have earned **Saltwater Grille** (231 Front St., South Portland, 207/799-5400, www.saltwatergrille. com, from 11:30am daily, dinner entrées $13-30) an excellent reputation. Dine inside or on the waterfront deck.

If you're venturing out to Cape Elizabeth, detour into **The Good Table** (527 Ocean House Rd./Rte. 77, Cape Elizabeth, 207/799-4663, www.thegoodtablerestaurant.net, 8am-9pm Tues.-Sun., entrées $11-20). Lisa Kostopoulos's popular local restaurant serves home-style favorites as well as Greek specialties.

Dine al fresco at **The Well at Jordan's Farm** (21 Wells Rd., Cape Elizabeth, 207/831-9350, 5pm-9pm Wed.-Sat., $18-25), where Jason Williams, a Culinary Institute of America grad, creates dinners from the farm's bounty and other ingredients sourced locally. Everything is made from scratch. Seating is on picnic tables

on the lawn and in a gazebo or at the four-stool kitchen bar. In an interesting twist, all prices on the four-item menu are suggested. Cash only.

Sea Glass (40 Bowery Beach Rd./Rte. 77, Cape Elizabeth, 207/299-3134, entrées $23-34), at the Inn by the Sea, is a sleeper. Chef Mitchell Kaldrovich serves Maine-inspired fare with an Argentinian accent; his gaucho steak and his paella are each worth the trip, as is the ocean-view setting. Dine indoors or on the deck.

Every Mainer has a favorite lobster eatery (besides home), but **The Lobster Shack** (222 Two Lights Rd., Cape Elizabeth, 207/799-1677, www.lobstershacktwolights.com, 11am-8pm daily late Mar.-mid-Oct.) tops an awful lot of lists. Seniority helps—it has been here since the 1920s. There is scenery as well: a panoramic vista in the shadow of Cape Elizabeth Light. The menu has seafood galore along with burgers and hot dogs for those who'd rather not have lobster. Opt for a sunny day; the lighthouse's foghorn can kill your conversation when the fog rolls in.

INFORMATION AND SERVICES

The **Visitor Information Center of the Convention and Visitors Bureau of Greater Portland** (14 Ocean Gateway Pier, 207/772-5800, www.visitportland.com) has info and public restrooms. The **Portland Downtown District** (207/772-6828, www.portlandmaine. com) has a useful website.

Check out the **Portland Public Library** (5 Monument Sq., 207/871-1700, www.portlandlibrary.com).

In the Old Port area, you'll find **public restrooms** at the Visitor Information Center (14 Ocean Gateway Pier), Spring Street parking garage (45 Spring St.), Fore Street Parking Garage (419 Fore St.), and Casco Bay Lines ferry terminal (Commercial St. and Franklin St.). On Congress Street, find restrooms at

Portland City Hall (389 Congress St.) and the Portland Public Library (5 Monument Sq.). In Midtown, head for the Cumberland County Civic Center (1 Civic Center Sq.). In the West End, use Maine Medical Center (22 Bramhall St.).

GETTING THERE AND AROUND

Portland is about 100 miles or two hours via I-95 from Boston, although during peak travel periods it can take longer because of congestion and toll lines. It's about 26 miles or 45 minutes via Route 1 from Kennebunk. It's about 17 miles or 20 minutes via Route 295 to Freeport.

The ultraclean and comfortable **Portland Transportation Center** (100 Thompson Point Rd., 207/828-3939) is the base for **Concord Coachlines** (800/639-3317, www.concord-coachlines.com) and the **Amtrak Downeaster** (800/872-7245, www.amtrakdowneaster.com). Parking is $3 per day, and the terminal has free coffee, free newspapers (while they last), and vending machines. The **Metro** (207/774-0351, www.gpmetrobus.net $1.50/ride, $5/day pass, exact change required) stops here and connects with **Portland International Jetport** (207/774-7301, www.portlandjetport.org), **Greyhound Bus** (www.greyhound.com), and **Casco Bay Lines ferry service** (www.cascobaylines.com). Taxis charge $1.90 for the first 0.1 mile plus $0.30 for each additional 0.1 mile; minimum fare is $5; airport fares add $1.50 surcharge.

Parking

Street parking (meters or pay stations) is $1 per hour. Parking garages and lots are strategically situated all over downtown Portland, particularly in the Old Port and near the civic center. Some lots accept Park and Shop stickers, each valid for one free hour, from participating merchants. A day of parking generally runs $8-16. The Casco Bay Lines website (www.cascobaylines.com) has a very useful parking map listing parking lots and garages and their fees.

For winter parking-ban information, call 207/879-0300.

Casco Bay Islands

Casco Bay is dotted with so many islands that an early explorer thought there must be at least one for every day of the year and so dubbed them the Calendar Islands. Truthfully, there aren't quite that many, even if you count all the ledges that appear at low tide. No matter; the islands are as much a part of Portland life as the Old Port.

Casco Bay Lines (207/774-7871, www.cascobaylines.com) is the islands' lifeline, providing car and passenger service daily in summer. For an island taster, take the daily mail-boat run. Indeed, on hot days it may seem as if half the city's population is hopping a ferry to enjoy the cool breezes and calming views.

PEAKS ISLAND

Peaks Island is a mere 20-minute ferry ride from downtown Portland, so it's no surprise that it has the largest year-round population. Historically a popular vacation spot—two lodges were built for Civil War veterans—it's now an increasingly popular suburb.

Although you can walk the island's perimeter in 3-4 hours, the best way to see it is via bike (extra ferry cost $6.50 adults, $3.25 children), pedaling around clockwise. It can take less than an hour to do the five-mile island circuit, but plan to relax on the beach, savor the views, and visit the museums. Rental bikes are available on the island from Brad Burkholder at **Brad and Wyatt's Bike Shop** (115 Island Ave.,

Peaks Island, 207/766-5631, 10am-6pm daily, $15 per day, hourly rentals available).

Another way to see the island is on a golf-cart tour with **Island Tours** (207/653-2549, www.peaksislandtours.com, $18 adults, $12 children), which offers a variety of 90-minute island tours.

Civil War buffs have two museums worth visiting. The **Fifth Maine Regiment Center** (45 Seashore Ave., Peaks Island, 207/766-3330, www.fifthmainemuseum.org, noon-4pm Mon.-Fri., 11am-4pm Sat.-Sun. July 1-early Sept., 11am-4pm Sat.-Sun. late May-July 1 and early Sept.-mid-Oct., $5 donation) is a Queen Anne-style cottage built by Civil War veterans in 1888 that now houses exhibits on the war and island history. Just a few steps away is the **Eighth Maine Regimental Memorial** (13 Eighth Maine Ave., Peaks Island, 207/766-5086, www.eighthmaine.com, 11am-4pm Tues.-Sat. July 1-early Sept., $5 requested donation). Tours detail the building's fascinating history and its collection of artifacts pertaining to the Eighth Maine as well as material on the island, World War II, and more. Rustic lodging is available.

Another museum perhaps worthy of a visit just for its quirkiness is the **Umbrella Cover Museum** (207/766-4496, www.umbrellacover-museum.org, call for hours, donation), where owner Nancy 3. Hoffman (yes, 3) displays her Guinness World Record collection.

Accommodations

The **Inn on Peaks Island** (33 Island Ave., 207/766-5100, www.innonpeaks.com, $200-300) overlooks the ferry dock and has jaw-dropping sunset views over the Portland skyline; no island roughing it here. The spacious cottage-style suites have fireplaces, sitting areas, and whirlpool baths.

On the other end of the Peaks Island luxury scale is the extremely informal and communal **Eighth Maine Living Museum and Lodge** (13

Eighth Maine Ave., 207/766-5086, mid-May-mid-Sept., 914/237-3165 off-season, www.eighthmaine.com, $99-299), a rustic shorefront living-history lodge overlooking White Head Passage. Shared baths and a huge shared kitchen allow you to rusticate in much the same manner as the Civil War vets who built this place in 1891 with a gift from a veteran who had won the Louisiana Lottery.

Food

Both **The Cockeyed Gull** (78 Island Ave., 207/766-2880, www.cockeyedgull.com, 11:30am-9pm daily, entrées $10-27) and the **Shipyard Brewhaus** (33 Island Ave., www.innonpeaks.com, entrées $9-20) have inside dining as well as outdoor tables with water views.

GREAT CHEBEAGUE

Everyone calls Great Chebeague just "Chebeague" (shuh-BIG). Yes, there's a Little Chebeague, but it's a state-owned park and no one lives there. Chebeague is the largest of the bay's islands—4.5 miles long by 1.5 miles wide—and the relatively level terrain makes it easy to get around. Don't plan to bring a car; it's too complicated to arrange. You can bike the leisurely 10-mile circuit of the island in a couple of hours, but unless you're in a hurry, allow time to relax and enjoy your visit.

If the tide is right, cross the sand spit from The Hook and explore **Little Chebeague.** Start out about two hours before low tide (preferably around new moon or full moon, when the most water drains away) and plan to be back on Chebeague no later than two hours after low tide.

Back on Great Chebeague, when you're ready for a swim, head for **Hamilton Beach,** a beautiful small stretch of sand lined with dune grass and not far from the Chebeague Island Inn. Also on this part of the island is **East End Point,** with a spectacular panoramic view of Halfway Rock and the bay.

Chebeague Transportation Company, from Cousins Island, Yarmouth, also serves the island. Its boats dock near Chebeague Island Inn, which is within walking distance of Calder's Clam Shack.

Accommodations

Get that old-timey island experience at the **Chebeague Island Inn** (61 South Rd., Chebeague Island, 207/846-5155, www.chebeagueislandinn.com, from $250), a nicely updated historical inn that charms guests with an artsy spirit and comforts them with down duvets and fancy sheets. The inn's dining room serves all meals. Some rooms have shared baths.

Food

Visitors to Chebeague Island have two food choices. For simple home-cooked fare, head to **Calder's Clam Shack** (108 North Rd., Chebeague Island, 207/846-5046, www.caldersclamshack.com, 11:30am-8pm Tues.-Sun.), a takeout serving burgers, pizza, chowders, salad, sandwiches, and of course, fried seafood. On the fancier side is **Chebeague Island Inn** (61 South Rd., Chebeague Island, 207/846-5155, www.chebeagueislandinn.com, 7am-9pm). Dinner entrées, such as an organic cheeseburger and butter-poached lobster, run $16-38.

EAGLE ISLAND

Seventeen-acre Eagle Island (207/624-6080, www.pearyeagleisland.org, 10am-5pm mid-June-early Sept.) juts out of Casco Bay, rising to a rocky promontory 40 feet above the crashing surf. On the bluff's crest, Robert Edwin Peary, the first man to lead a party to the North Pole without the use of mechanical or electrical devices, built his dream home. It's now a state historic site that's accessible via excursion boats from Portland or Freeport. The half-day trip usually includes a narrated cruise to the island and time to tour the house, filled with Peary family artifacts, and wander the nature trails. Trails are usually closed until approximately mid-July to protect nesting eider ducks.

Peary envisioned the island's rocky bluff as a ship's prow and built his house to resemble a pilot house. Wherever possible, he used indigenous materials from the island in the construction, including timber drift, fallen trees, beach rocks, and cement mixed with screened beach sand and small pebbles. From the library, Peary corresponded with world leaders, adventurers, and explorers such as Teddy Roosevelt, the Wright brothers, Roald Amundsen, and Ernest Shackleton, and planned his expeditions. Peary reached the North Pole on April 6, 1909, and his wife, Josephine, was on Eagle Island when she received word via telegraph of her husband's accomplishment. After Peary's death in 1920, the family continued to spend summers on Eagle until Josephine's death in 1955. The family then decided to donate the island to the state of Maine.

Freeport

Freeport has a special claim to historic fame—it's the place where Maine parted company from Massachusetts in 1820. The documents were signed on March 15, making Maine its own state.

At the height of the local mackerel-packing industry, countless tons of the bony fish were shipped out of South Freeport, often in ships built on the shores of the Harraseeket River. Splendid relics of the shipbuilders' era still line the streets of South Freeport, and no architecture buff should miss a walk, cycle, or drive through the village. Even downtown Freeport still reflects the shipbuilders' craft, with contemporary shops tucked in and around handsome historic houses. Some have been converted to bed-and-breakfasts, others are boutiques, and one even disguises the local McDonald's franchise.

Today, Freeport is best known as the mecca for the shop-till-you-drop set. The hub, of course, is sporting giant L. L. Bean, which has been here since 1912 when founder Leon Leonwood Bean began making his trademark hunting boots (and also unselfishly handed out hot tips on where the fish were biting). More than 120 retail operations now fan out from that epicenter, and you can find almost anything in Freeport, except maybe a convenient parking spot in midsummer.

When you tire of shopping, you can always find quiet refuge in the town's preserves and parks along with plenty of local color at the Town Wharf in the still honest-to-goodness fishing village of South Freeport.

An orientation note: Don't be surprised to receive directions (particularly for South Freeport) relative to "the Big Indian"—a

GREATER PORTLAND

© HILARY NANGLE

Admiral Robert Edwin Peary's Eagle Island home is open to visitors who arrive via Atlantic Seal Cruises.

© HILARY NANGLE

GREATER PORTLAND

Giant outdoor retailer and outfitter
L. L. Bean put Freeport on America's
shopping map.

40-foot-tall landmark at the junction of Route
1 and South Freeport Road. If you stop at the
Maine Visitor Information Center in Yarmouth
and continue on Route 1 toward Freeport, you
can't miss it.

SHOPPING

Logically, this category must come first in any
discussion of Freeport, since shopping is the
biggest game in town. It's pretty much a given
that anyone who visits Freeport intends to
darken the door of at least one shop.

◖ L. L. Bean

If you visit only one store in Freeport, it's
likely to be "Bean's." The whole world beats
a path to L. L. Bean (95 Main St./Rte. 1,
207/865-4761 or 800/341-4341, www.ll-
bean.com)—or so it seems in July-August

and December. Established as a hunting and
fishing supply shop, this giant sports outfitter now sells everything from kids' clothing
to cookware on its ever-expanding downtown campus. Look for the outlet store—
a great source for deals on equipment and
clothing—in the Village Square Shops across
Main Street.

Until the 1970s, Bean's remained a rustic
store with a creaky staircase and a closet-size
women's department. Then a few other merchants began arriving, Bean's expanded, and a
feeding frenzy followed. The Bean reputation
rests on a savvy staff, high quality, an admirable
environmental consciousness, and a no-ques-
tions-asked return policy. Bring the kids—for
the indoor trout pond and the aquarium-view-
ing bulb, the clean restrooms, and the "real
deal" outlet store. The store's open-round-the-
clock policy has become its signature; if you
show up at 2am, you'll have much of the store
to yourself, and you may even spy vacationing
celebrities or the rock stars who often visit after
Portland shows.

Outlets and Specialty Stores

After Bean's, it's up to your whims and your
wallet. The stores stretch for several miles up
and down Main Street and along many side
streets. Pick up a copy of the *Official Map and
Visitor Guide* at any of the shops or restaurants, at one of the visitor kiosks, or at the Hose
Tower Information Center (23 Depot St., two
blocks east of L. L. Bean). All the big names are
here, as are plenty of little ones. Don't overlook
the small shops tucked on the side streets.

SIGHTS
Desert of Maine

Okay, so maybe it's a bit hokey, but talk about
sands of time: More than 10,000 years ago, gla-
ciers covered the region surrounding the Desert
of Maine (95 Desert Rd., 207/865-6962, www.

desertofmaine.com, early May-mid-Oct., $10.50 adults, $7.75 ages 13-16, $6.75 ages 5-12). When they receded, they scoured the landscape, pulverizing rocks and leaving behind a sandy residue that was covered by a thin layer of topsoil. Jump forward to 1797, when William Tuttle bought 300 acres and moved his family here along with his house and barn and cleared the land. Now jump forward again to the present and tour where a once-promising farmland has become a desert wasteland. The 30-minute guided safari-style tram tours combine history, geology, and environmental science and an opportunity for children to hunt for "gems" in the sand. Decide for yourself: Is the desert a natural phenomenon? A human-made disaster? Or does the truth lie somewhere in between?

Harrington House and Pettengill Farm

A block south of L. L. Bean is the Harrington House (45 Main St./Rte. 1, 207/865-3170, www.freeporthistoricalsociety.org, 10am-5pm Mon.-Fri., free), home base of the Freeport Historical Society. You can pick up walking maps detailing Freeport's architecture for a small fee. Displays pertaining to Freeport's history and occasionally exhibits by local artists are presented in two rooms in the restored 1830 Enoch Harrington House, a property on the National Register of Historic Places.

Also listed on the register is the society's Pettengill Farm, a 19th-century saltwater farm comprising a circa-1810 saltbox-style house, woods, orchards, a salt marsh, and lovely perennial gardens. The farmhouse is open only during the annual Pettengill Farm Days in the fall, but the grounds are open at all times. From Main Street, take Bow Street 1.5 miles and turn right onto Pettengill Road. Park at the gate, and then walk along the dirt road for about 15 minutes to the farmhouse.

Eartha

She's a worldly woman, that Eartha. The **DeLorme Mapping Co.** (Rte. 1, Yarmouth, 207/846-7000, www.delorme.com/about/eartha.aspx) is home to the world's largest rotating and revolving globe, a three-story-tall spherical scale model of Earth. Eartha, as she's known, measures 41 feet in diameter with a 130-foot waist and weighs nearly three tons. She spins in DeLorme's glass-walled lobby, making her visible to passersby, but she's best appreciated up close and, well, as personal as you can get with a monstrous globe. Each continent is detailed with mountains and landforms, vegetation and civilization. She can be viewed 9:30am-5pm Monday-Friday. Take Route 1 south from downtown Freeport to the I-295 Exit 17 interchange; DeLorme is on the left.

Blueberry Pond Observatory

Prepare to be wowed by the night sky at the Blueberry Pond Observatory (355 Libby Road, Pownal, 207/688-4410, www.blueberryobservatory.com), where you'll get exclusive viewings of constellations, planets, nebulas, asteroids, and galaxies. Guided two-hour tours, which include extensive viewing and digital astronomy pictures, cost $140 for the first adult and $20 for each additional adult; children 12 and younger are free. One-hour tours, which don't include photography, are half the cost.

ENTERTAINMENT

Shopping seems to be more than enough entertainment for most of Freeport's visitors, but don't miss the **L. L. Bean Summer Concert Series** (800/341-4341, ext. 37222). At 7:30pm most Saturdays early July-Labor Day weekend, Bean's hosts free big-name family-oriented events in Discovery Park, in the Bean's complex (95 Main St./Rte. 1). Arrive early—these concerts are *very* popular—and bring a blanket or a folding chair.

RECREATION
Parks, Preserves, and Other Attractions
MAST LANDING SANCTUARY

Take precautions against disease-carrying mosquitoes and ticks when exploring preserves. Just one mile from downtown Freeport, Mast Landing Audubon Sanctuary (Upper Mast Landing Rd., 207/781-2330, www.maineaudubon.org, free) is a reprieve from the crowds. Situated at the head of the tide on the Harraseeket River estuary, the 140-acre preserve has 3.5 miles of signed trails weaving through an apple orchard, across fields, and through pines and hemlocks. The name? Ages ago it was the source of masts for the Royal Navy. To find it, take Bow Street (across from L. L. Bean) one mile to Upper Mast Landing Road and turn left. The sanctuary is 0.25 mile along on the left.

WOLFE'S NECK WOODS STATE PARK

Five miles of easy to moderate trails meander through 233-acre Wolfe's Neck Woods State Park (Wolfe's Neck Rd., 207/865-4465, www.parksandlands.com, $4.50 nonresident adults, $3 Maine resident adults, $1 ages 5-11), just a few minutes' cycle or drive from downtown Freeport. You'll need a trail map, available near the parking area. The easiest route (partly wheelchair accessible) is the Shoreline Walk, about 0.75 mile, starting near the salt marsh and skirting Casco Bay. Sprinkled along the trails are helpful interpretive panels explaining various points of natural history—bog life, osprey nesting, glaciation, erosion, and tree decay. Guided tours are offered at 2pm daily mid-July-late August, weather permitting. Leashed pets are allowed. Adjacent **Googins Island,** an osprey sanctuary, is off-limits. From downtown Freeport, follow Bow Street (across from L. L. Bean) for 2.25 miles; turn right onto Wolfe's Neck Road (also called Wolf Neck Rd.) and go another 2.25 miles.

WOLFE'S NECK FARM

Kids love Wolfe's Neck Farm (10 Burnett Rd., 207/865-4469, www.wolfesneckfarm.org), a 626-acre saltwater farm dedicated to sustainable agriculture and environmental education. Visit with farm animals and enjoy the farm's trails and varied habitats—fields, forests, seashore, and gardens—at no charge.

WINSLOW MEMORIAL PARK

Bring a kite. Bring a beach blanket. Bring a picnic. Bring a boat. Bring binoculars. Heck, bring a tent. Freeport's 90-acre oceanfront town-owned playground, Winslow Memorial Park (207/865-4198, www.freeportmaine.com, $3) has a spectacular setting on a peninsula extending into island-studded Casco Bay. Facilities include a boat launch ($3-5), a campground ($23-33, no hookups), a fishing pier, a volleyball court, scenic trails, a playground, restrooms, picnic facilities, and a sandy beach—the best swimming is at high tide, and there is no lifeguard. On Thursday evenings in July-August, local bands play. The park is 5.5 miles from downtown. Head south on Route 1 to the Big Indian (you'll know it when you see it), go left on the South Freeport Road for one mile to Staples Point Road, and follow it to the end.

BRADBURY MOUNTAIN STATE PARK

Six miles from the hubbub of Freeport you're in tranquil, wooded 590-acre Bradbury Mountain State Park (Rte. 9, Pownal, 207/688-4712, www.parksandlands.com, $4.50 nonresident adults, $3 Maine resident adults, $1 ages 5-11), with facilities for picnicking, hiking, mountain biking, and rustic camping, but no swimming. Pick up a trail map at the gate and take the easy 0.4-mile round-trip Mountain Trail to the 485-foot summit, with superb views east to the ocean and southeast to Portland. It's gorgeous in fall. Or take the Tote Road Trail, on the western side of the park, where the ghost of Samuel Bradbury allegedly occasionally brings a chill to hikers in a hemlock grove. A playground keeps the littlest tykes happy. The camping fee is $19 per site for non-residents, $11 for residents. The park season is May 15-October 15, but there's winter access for cross-country skiing. From Route 1, cross over I-95 at Exit 20 and continue west on Pownal Road to Route 9 and head south.

PINELAND FARMS

Once a home for Maine's mentally disabled citizens, the 5,000-acre Pineland (15 Farm View Dr., New Gloucester, 207/688-4539, www.pinelandfarms.org, $5) campus was closed in 1996. Now the foundation-owned property comprises 19 buildings and 5,000 acres of farmland, and much of it is open for recreation. Walk or ski the trails, sight birds in the fields and woods, watch cheese being made, stroll through the garden, fish the pond or skate on it in winter, play tennis, go mountain biking or orienteering, or even take a horseback-riding lesson. It's a vast outdoor playground, but your first stop should be the market and visitors center (8am-7pm daily) to see a list of any events (frequent ones include guided farm tours and family experiences), pick up maps, pay any necessary fees, shop for farm-fresh products, or even grab lunch or snacks. Dogs are not allowed.

◖ L. L. Bean Outdoor Discovery Schools

Since the early 1980s, the sports outfitter's Outdoor Discovery Schools (888/552-3261, www.llbean.com) have trained thousands of outdoors enthusiasts to improve their skills in fly-fishing, archery, hiking, canoeing, sea kayaking, winter camping, cross-country skiing, orienteering, and even outdoor photography. Here's a deal that requires no planning. **Walk-on Adventures** ($20, includes equipment) provide 1.5-2.5-hour lessons in sports

such as kayak touring, fly casting, archery, clay shooting, snowshoeing, and cross-country skiing. All of the longer fee programs, plus canoeing and camping trips, require preregistration well in advance. Some of the lectures, seminars, and demonstrations held in Freeport are free, and a regular catalog lists the schedule. Bean's waterfront **Flying Point Paddling Center** hosts many of the kayaking, saltwater fly-fishing, and guiding programs and is home to the annual **PaddleSports Festival** in June, with free demonstrations, seminars, vendors, lessons, and more.

Boat Excursions

Atlantic Seal Cruises (Town Wharf, South Freeport, 207/865-6112 or 877/285-7325, www.atlanticsealcruises.com), owned and operated by Captain Tom Ring, makes two 2.5-hour cruises ($35 adults, $25 ages 5-12, $20 ages 1-4) daily to 17-acre **Eagle Island** (www.pearyeagleisland.org), a State Historic Site once owned by Admiral Robert Peary, the North Pole explorer. The trip includes a lobstering demonstration (except Sunday, when lobstering is banned). Once a week he offers a daylong excursion to **Seguin Island** ($55 ages 10 and older, $40 kids), off the Phippsburg Peninsula, where you can climb the light tower and see Maine's only first-order Fresnel lens, the largest on the coast.

Kayak, Canoe, and Bike Rentals

Ring's Marine Service (Smelt Brook Rd., South Freeport, 207/865-6143, www.ringsmarineservice.com) rents single kayaks for $35, tandems for $50, and canoes for $30 per day, with longer-term rentals and delivery available. Bikes are $18 for a half day.

ACCOMMODATIONS

If you'd prefer to drop where you shop, Freeport has plentiful accommodations. Rates listed are for peak season.

Downtown

One of Freeport's pioneering bed-and-breakfasts is on the main drag but away from much of the traffic in a restored house where Arctic explorer Admiral Donald MacMillan once lived. The 19th-century **White Cedar Inn** (178 Main St., 207/865-9099 or 800/853-1269, www.whitecedarinn.com, $180-350) has seven attractive guest rooms and a two-bedroom suite with antiques, air-conditioning, and Wi-Fi; some have gas fireplaces, and one has a TV and accepts dogs ($25, includes bowls, quilt, and towel). The full breakfast will power you through a day of shopping.

Two blocks north of L. L. Bean, the **(Harraseeket Inn** (162 Main St., 207/865-9377 or 800/342-6423, www.harraseeketinn.com, $195-315) is a splendid 84-room country inn with an indoor pool, cable TV, air-conditioning, phones, and Wi-Fi; many rooms have fireplaces and hot tubs. One room is decorated with Thomas Moser furnishings; otherwise decor is colonial reproduction in the two historical buildings and a modern addition. The inn is especially accessible, so it's a prime choice for anyone with mobility issues. Rates include a hot-and-cold buffet breakfast and afternoon tea with finger sandwiches and sweets—a refreshing break. Pets are permitted in some guest rooms for $25, which includes a dog bed, a small can of food, a treat, and dishes. Ask about packages, which offer great value. Children 12 and younger stay free. The inn is home to two excellent dining venues, and it's long been a leader in the farm-to-table movement.

Three blocks south of L. L. Bean on a quiet side street shared with a couple of other bed-and-breakfasts is **The James Place Inn** (11 Holbrook St., 207/865-4486 or 800/964-9086, www.jamesplaceinn.com, $165-195). Innkeepers Robin and Tori Baron welcome guests to seven comfortable guest rooms, all with air-conditioning, Wi-Fi, TVs and DVD players; a few have double whirlpool tubs, and one has a private deck and fireplace. If the weather is fine, enjoy breakfast on the inn's deck. After shopping, collapse on the hammock for two.

Beyond Downtown

Three miles north of downtown is the **Maine Idyll** (1411 Rte. 1, 207/865-4201, www.maineidyll.com, $70-125), a tidy cottage colony operated by the Marstaller family for three generations. It is a retro throwback and a find for budget-bound travelers. Twenty studio to three-bedroom pine-paneled cottages are tucked under the trees. The Ritz this is not, but all have refrigerators, fireplaces, and TVs, and most have limited cooking facilities. Wi-Fi is available near the office. A light breakfast is included. Well-behaved pets are welcome for $4.

The family-run **(Casco Bay Inn** (107 Rte. 1, 207/865-4925 or 800/570-4970, www.cascobayinn.com, $105-135) is a bit fancier than most motels. It has a pine-paneled lounge with a fieldstone fireplace and a guest Internet station as well as Wi-Fi throughout. The spacious guest rooms have double sinks in the bath area, and some have a refrigerator and a microwave. A continental breakfast with a newspaper is included.

Camping

For anyone seeking peace, quiet, and low-tech camping in a spectacular setting, **Recompence Shore Campsites** (134 Burnett Rd., 207/865-9307, www.freeportcamping.com, $26-46) is it. Part of Wolfe's Neck Farm foundation, the eco-sensitive campground has 118 wooded tent sites and a few hookups, many on the farm's three-mile-long Casco Bay shorefront. Kayak, canoe, and bike rentals are available; swimming depends on the tides. Facilities include a playground and snack bar with Wi-Fi. Take Bow Street (across from L. L. Bean) to Wolfe's Neck Road, turn right, go 1.6 miles, then turn left on

Burnett Road. Three pet-friendly oceanfront camping cabins are $115-150, plus $10 per pet.

FOOD

Freeport has an ever-increasing number of places to eat, but there are nowhere near enough to satisfy hungry crowds at peak dining hours on busy days. Go early or late for lunch, and make reservations for dinner. Days and hours are for peak season, but it's always wise to verify.

Local Flavors

South of downtown, **Royal River Natural Foods** (443 Rte. 1, 207/865-0046) has a small selection of prepared foods, including soups, salads, and sandwiches, and there is a seating area.

Craving a proper British tea? **Jacqueline's Tea Room** (201 Main St., 207/865-2123, www.jacquelinestearoom.com) serves a four-course tea for about $25 pp in an elegant setting. Seatings for the two-hour indulgence are between 11am and 1pm Tuesday-Saturday.

At the Big Indian **Old World Gourmet Deli and Wine Shop** (117 Rte. 1, 207/865-4477, www.oldworldgourmet.com), the offerings are just as advertised, with sandwiches, soups, salads, and prepared foods. There are a few tables inside, but it's mostly a to-go place.

Casual Dining

The Harraseeket Inn (162 Main St., 207/865-9377 or 800/342-6423) has two restaurants. The woodsy-themed ◖ **Broad Arrow Tavern** (162 Main St., 207/865-9377 or 800/342-6423, from 11:30am daily $10-30), just two blocks north of L. L. Bean but seemingly a world away, is a perfect place to escape shopping crowds and madness. The food is terrific, with everything made from organic and naturally raised foods. Can't decide? Opt for the extensive all-you-can-eat lunch buffet ($17) that highlights a bit of everything. In early 2013, the inn teamed with the Maine Organic Farmers and Gardeners Association and the Maine Farmland Trust and completely renovated and enlarged its main restaurant, renaming it **Maine Harvest** (5:30pm-9pm daily, dinner entrées $20-38). The restaurant showcases not only farm-to-table fare but also the people who make it happen and the story behind preserving and cultivating organic farmland in the state. The menu emphasizes creative pairings and artistic presentations. Brunch (11:45am-2pm Sun., $26) is a seemingly endless buffet, with whole poached salmon and Belgian waffles among the highlights.

Good wine and fine martinis are what reels them into **Conundrum** (117 Rte. 1, 207/865-0303, from 4:30pm Tues.-Sat., $12-25), near Freeport's Big Indian, but the food is worth noting too. Dozens of wines by the glass, more than 20 martinis, and 20 champagnes will keep most oenophiles happy. The food, varying from pâtés and cheese platters to cheeseburgers and maple-barbecued chicken, helps keep patrons sober.

Ethnic Fare

Dine indoors or out on the tree-shaded patio at **Azure Italian Café** (123 Main St., 207/865-1237, www.azurecafe.com, from 11:30am daily). Go light, mixing selections from antipasto, *insalate,* and *zuppa* choices, or savor the heartier entrées ($18-33). The service is pleasant, and the indoor dining areas are accented by well-chosen contemporary Maine artwork. Live jazz is a highlight some evenings.

Down the side street across from Azure is **Mediterranean Grill** (10 School St., 207/865-1688, www.mediterraneangrill.biz, 11:30am-9pm daily, entrées $16-25). Because it's off Main Street, the Cigri family's excellent Turkish-Mediterranean restaurant rarely gets the crowds. House specialties such as moussaka, lamb chops, and *tiropetes* augment a full range of kebab and vegetarian choices. Or

GREATER PORTLAND

simply make a meal of the appetizers—the platters are meals in themselves. Sandwiches and wraps are available at lunch.

Two surprisingly good, easy-on-the-budget Asian restaurants share a building on the south end of town. **China Rose** (23 Main St., 207/865-6886, 11am-9:30pm daily, entrées $10-16) serves Szechuan, Mandarin, and Hunan specialties in a pleasant first-floor dining area. Upstairs is **Miyako** (207/865-6888, 11am-9:30pm daily $6-20), with an extensive sushi bar menu; it also serves other Japanese specialties, including tempura, teriyaki, *nabemono,* and noodle dishes. Luncheon specials are available at both.

Good food and attentive service has made **Thai Garden** (491 Rte. 1, 207/865-6005, 11am-9pm daily, $8-15) an ever-popular choice.

Lobster

In South Freeport, order lobster in the rough at **Harraseeket Lunch and Lobster Company** (36 Main St., Town Wharf, South Freeport, lunch counter 207/865-4888, lobster pound 207/865-3535, 11am-8:45pm daily summer, 11am-7:45pm daily spring and fall, no credit cards). Grab a picnic table, place your order, and go at it. Be prepared for crowds and a wait in midsummer. Fried clams are particularly good here, and they're prepared either breaded or battered. BYOB.

Far more peaceful is **Day's Seafood Takeout** (1269 Rte. 1, Yarmouth, 207/836-3436, 11am-8pm daily), with a few picnic tables out back overlooking a tidal estuary.

INFORMATION AND SERVICES

Freeport Merchants Association (Hose Tower, 23 Depot St., 207/865-1212 or 800/865-1994, www.freeportusa.com) produces an invaluable foldout map-guide showing locations of all the shops, plus sites of lodgings, restaurants, visitor kiosks, pay phones, restrooms, and car and bike parking.

Just south of Freeport is the **Maine Visitor Information Center** (Rte. 1 at I-95 Exit 17, Yarmouth, 207/846-0833), part of the statewide tourism-information network. Also here are restrooms, phones, picnic tables, vending machines, and a dog-walking area.

GETTING THERE AND AROUND

Freeport is about 18 miles or 20 minutes via Route 295 from Portland. It's about 10 miles or 15 minutes via Route 295 to Brunswick.

Some **Amtrak Downeaster** (800/872-7245, www.thedowneaster.com) trains stop in Freeport.

www.moon.com

DESTINATIONS | ACTIVITIES | BLOGS | MAPS | BOOKS

MOON.COM is ready to help plan your next trip! Filled with fresh trip ideas and strategies, author interviews, informative travel blogs, a detailed map library, and descriptions of all the Moon guidebooks, Moon.com is all you need to get out and explore the world—or even places in your own backyard. While at Moon.com, sign up for our monthly e-newsletter for updates on new releases, travel tips, and expert advice from our on-the-go Moon authors. As always, when you travel with Moon, expect an experience that is uncommon and truly unique.

KEEP UP WITH MOON ON FACEBOOK AND TWITTER
JOIN THE MOON PHOTO GROUP ON FLICKR

MAP SYMBOLS

▦ Expressway	€ Highlight	✗ Airfield	⚷ Golf Course
⋯⋯ Primary Road	○ City/Town	✈ Airport	▣ Parking Area
━━ Secondary Road	◉ State Capital	▲ Mountain	⬛ Archaeological Site
▪▪▪ Unpaved Road	⊛ National Capital	✦ Unique Natural Feature	ᵻ Church
------ Trail	★ Point of Interest		⬚ Gas Station
⋯⋯ Ferry	• Accommodation	⚑ Waterfall	⬡ Glacier
⊸⊸ Railroad	▾ Restaurant/Bar	▲ Park	⬚ Mangrove
▦ Pedestrian Walkway	▪ Other Location	▣ Trailhead	▦ Reef
⬛ Stairs	⋀ Campground	⅀ Skiing Area	▦ Swamp

CONVERSION TABLES

$°C = (°F - 32) / 1.8$
$°F = (°C \times 1.8) + 32$
1 inch = 2.54 centimeters (cm)
1 foot = 0.304 meters (m)
1 yard = 0.914 meters
1 mile = 1.6093 kilometers (km)
1 km = 0.6214 miles
1 fathom = 1.8288 m
1 chain = 20.1168 m
1 furlong = 201.168 m
1 acre = 0.4047 hectares
1 sq km = 100 hectares
1 sq mile = 2.59 square km
1 ounce = 28.35 grams
1 pound = 0.4536 kilograms
1 short ton = 0.90718 metric ton
1 short ton = 2,000 pounds
1 long ton = 1.016 metric tons
1 long ton = 2,240 pounds
1 metric ton = 1,000 kilograms
1 quart = 0.94635 liters
1 US gallon = 3.7854 liters
1 Imperial gallon = 4.5459 liters
1 nautical mile = 1.852 km

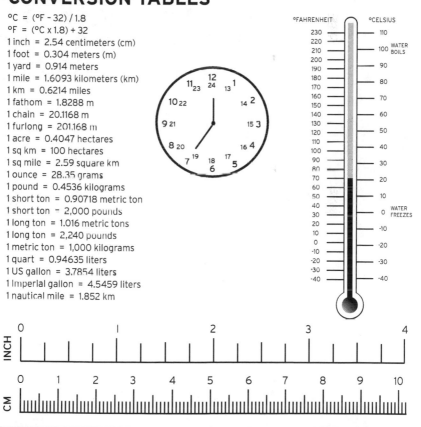

MOON SPOTLIGHT MAINE'S
  SOUTHERN COAST
Avalon Travel
a member of the Perseus Books Group
1700 Fourth Street
Berkeley, CA 94710, USA
www.moon.com

Editors: Leah Gordon, Erin Raber
Series Manager: Kathryn Ettinger
Copy Editor: Laurel Robinson
Graphics Coordinator: Elizabeth Jang
Production Coordinator: Elizabeth Jang
Cover Designer: Kathryn Osgood
Map Editor: Mike Morgenfeld
Cartographer: Chris Henrick

ISBN: 978-1-61238-579-2

Text © 2013 by Hilary Nangle.
Maps © 2013 by Avalon Travel.
All rights reserved.

Some photos and illustrations are used by permission
and are the property of the original copyright
owners.

Front cover photo: lobster buoys in Portland, Maine
© John Alphonse | Dreamstime.com

Title Page photo: Portland Head Light © alessandro
0770/123rf.com

Printed in the United States

Moon Spotlight and the Moon logo are the property
of Avalon Travel. All other marks and logos depicted
are the property of the original owners. All rights
reserved. No part of this book may be translated or
reproduced in any form, except brief extracts by a
reviewer for the purpose of a review, without written
permission of the copyright owner.

All recommendations, including those for sights,
activities, hotels, restaurants, and shops, are based
on each author's individual judgment. We do not
accept payment for inclusion in our travel guides,
and our authors don't accept free goods or services
in exchange for positive coverage.

Although every effort was made to ensure that
the information was correct at the time of going
to press, the author and publisher do not assume
and hereby disclaim any liability to any party for any
loss or damage caused by errors, omissions, or any
potential travel disruption due to labor or financial
difficulty, whether such errors or omissions result
from negligence, accident, or any other cause.

KEEPING CURRENT

If you have a favorite gem you'd like to see included in the next edition, or see anything
that needs updating, clarification, or correction, please drop us a line. Send your com-
ments via email to feedback@moon.com, or use the address above.

ABOUT THE AUTHOR

Hilary Nangle

Despite brief out-of-state interludes for college, grad school, and a stint as a ski bum, Hilary Nangle has never been able to resist the lure of her home state. She grew up on Maine's coast, spending much of each winter skiing in the western mountains. Her sense of wanderlust was ignited when she became a whitewater-rafting guide on the Kennebec River, which gave her a chance to explore the central and northern regions of the state. When she tired of her parents asking when she was going to get a *real job,* she drew on her writing skills and began seeking editorial work. She started out editing professional ski tour publications, and then became a managing editor for a food trade publication and later a features editor for a daily newspaper. She currently works as a freelance writer and editor.

Hilary never tires of exploring Maine, always seeking out the offbeat and quirky, and rarely resisting the invitation of a back road. To her husband's dismay, she inherited her grandmother's shopping gene and can't pass a used bookstore, artisans gallery, or antiques shop without browsing. She's equally curious about food and has never met a lobster she didn't like. Hilary still divides her year between the coast and the mountains, residing with her husband, photographer Tom Nangle, and their oversized dog. Both share her passions for long walks and Maine-made ice cream. To follow Hilary's travels, visit mainetravelmaven.com.